The turkey which really was a rooster!

And Tom's other stories from Africa

By Tom Hogan CSSp.

Dedication
*I dedicate this book to my family, confrères and friends
who have helped me in so many ways during my life.
Many of them came and visited me during my 31 years in Africa.*

Published April 2012 by CRM Publications Dublin.

ISBN: 978-0-9571557-1-8

Acknowledgements
Thanks to Anne Phelan, Maureen and Ruth Cassin, Tony and Patricia Hogan
for proof-reading; Mark Lawler, Noirin Phelan,
Tanya and Tamsin Hogan for their editing skills.
Illustration for the oral literature story is by Sarah Lawler.

Photo Credits:
Front Cover photo: 'Baobab Tree' by Pat Hogan
Cover design by Richard Kelly
Photo of author by Patrick Bolger

*(According to African legend, the baobab tree did not like the way God created it
and complained to God about this. It was then uprooted and planted upside down.
So that is why the baobab tree looks as if its roots are in the air!)*

Design, layout and printing
CRM Design +Print Ltd., Dublin 12.
01-429 0007

Table of Contents

Preface	5
About the author	6
Why read about Tom's life?	8
Map of Kenya	9

Part 1
MWATATE, THE TAITA HILLS, KENYA 1974-1982 — 11

Map of the Taita hills and surrounding area	11
Introduction	12
First Funeral	12
The Christmas Radio	13
Mwatate Parish and hot, hot plates	13
The WaTaita People	14
Refugees from Mozambique	15
The turkey which really was a rooster!	15
The washing of the feet	16
The man who rose from the dead	17
Measles outbreak	18
A charitable journey and a bottle of whiskey	19
The power of Holy Water	20
Dembwa Catholic Church	20
Mama Helena	21
The sleeping lion	21
Always turn left	22
Oral Literature; the monkey and the turtle	23
Birth stories	26
The curious case of the woman in the mirror	27
The ambulance that became a meat van!	28
New names for us: 'Wakio and Mwangeka'	28

Part 2
ST. MARY'S SCHOOL, NAIROBI 1982-1995

Introduction	32
The best in the world	32
Stories: Rapture Road	34
The octopus and its tentacles	34
"Thank you for wasting your time"	34
The dead body	34
A serious case of worms	35
The message in a bottle	35
The great April fool's gag	36
Camping adventures – the Surprise Club	37
Hippos run quickly!	38
Turkana odyssey, a hospital in a desert and a surprise birthday party	39
Lake Nakuru	43
Amboseli: kites, frights and cello players	44
Tsavo National Park – Baboons like crisps!	46
Tsavo adventure – Shake-down Cruise and Death Soup	47
Rumuruti camp: another use for a filing cabinet!	50
A few dirty words	50
Bike trek Safari	50
A story of bravery	52
A difficult case in discipline	52
Refugees – my new brother and sister	54
Our days at "Saints"	56

Part 3
BURA-TANA, GARISSA
1995-2004　　　　　　　　57

Bura-Tana – Introduction	58
Irrigation Settlement Schemes – and a new challenge	58
Women cannot speak when men are present	60
Rain Harvesting, the Bura-Tana Mechanics Club and the 10 second shower	61
The New Ten Commandments	63
Tunza Mtoto – Child Survival Programme	64
Our first Christmas in Bura-Tana	64
A parcel from Ireland, garlic worms and the Liquorice Allsorts cake	65
God sends us a hunter	65
Impregnated nets	67
A coffin made from doors	67
The Kibiriti kit – health in a match box	68
The Merry Go Round	69
A letter from Al Qaida	70
Can crocodiles see in the dark?	70
Dedeche	71
El Niño	71
The Somali	73
Educating Lucy	73
Stick your thumb in the crocodile's eye	74
The Christmas Crib	75
Dead woman in my jeep	76
The cabbage that became a flower	77
Visitors at night	78
Water, water everywhere and rain dams!	81
Mamoud Tom and the Hole in the Wall gang	82
A further lesson in generosity	82
Time to say goodbye to Bura-Tana and start a new venture	83
Animals visit our camp	84
The crocodile has eaten our dog	85
Policemen teach us how to be generous	86
More visitors to our camp and time to return home	87

Preface

A number of people have encouraged me to write down my stories from Africa. My friend Steven Clancy said to me on a number of occasions: "I have heard some interesting stories from you people and you should make a collection of stories about *you and your friends*". So, Steven, this is a start!

However, it was my grand-nephew, Christopher Phelan, who got me started when he said: *"You are repeating yourself. Write the stories down!"* So, Christopher and friends, here you are!

My grand-nephew Tom Behrens in Australia is responsible for the story about monkeys. He sent me a message asking if I knew any stories about monkeys. The "Oral Literature" story is my adaptation of a number of stories about monkeys that I have heard.

Tamsin Hogan spent one Easter with me helping me to write and tape record the stories. She asked me endless questions! Tamsin and her sister Tanya have been the editors and I thank them both for their encouragement and their efforts.

My brothers and sisters have always encouraged me to tell stories to their children and I thank them for that. Some of them used to read my letters to my nieces and nephews – maybe that's what created the expectation!

About the Author

Tom was born in Tramore, County Waterford, Ireland, in 1946. After completing his primary education at Christian Brothers School in Tramore, he attended secondary school in Rockwell College. While studying at Rockwell, Tom met and was influenced by priests and student priests who had worked as missionaries overseas. Tom became very interested in the idea of working overseas. After he finished school, he joined the Congregation of the Holy Spirit and completed his studies in Kilshane and Kimmage Manor, Dublin.

His first two years as a teacher were spent in Willow Park, Blackrock. Lessons learned from Fr Bob Stanley, the Principal were to prove very useful when Tom became Principal and Headmaster years later in Africa.

Tom was ordained in his home town of Tramore as a missionary priest in June 1972. This was the first ordination ever to take place in the Holy Cross Church Tramore, where he had been baptised, made his first Holy Communion and was confirmed.

The members of the Congregation are known as 'Spiritans' in Continental Europe and as either 'Spiritans' or 'Holy Ghost Fathers' in English-speaking countries. A Spiritan has the abbreviation 'C.S.Sp.' after his name. The Spiritans also have lay associate members, both men and women. Some of the associates are married and have children. Spiritans are known as people who will go anywhere they are

asked to, even when no one else will go there.

After ordination, Tom was faced with the task of choosing where to work as a missionary priest. Kenya, one of the countries where he was offered a position, was where he would spend thirty-one diverse years working in education.

For the first seven years, he lived in a rural area, teaching in a National Government school. He was then transferred to the Spiritan St. Mary's School in Nairobi, a large primary and secondary school. Tom became Principal of the primary school and was subsequently appointed Headmaster.

In 1995, Tom enrolled in a Masters in Health Promotion at the University of

London. He undertook research for his thesis in Bura-Tana, Garissa, Kenya and took a new post in this area the following year.

Garissa is the largest diocese in Kenya and comprises one sixth of the landmass of Kenya. This semi-arid area is sparsely populated, averaging one person per square kilometer. There is little access to healthcare in Tana River, with one doctor for a quarter of a million people. There is little public transport and vehicles are not allowed to travel at night.

On arrival in Bura-Tana, health promotion was identified as an area where significant improvements could be made, especially in dealing with the control of the AIDS epidemic and specifically with a Child Survival Programme. Tom was appointed as the Co-ordinator of 'Tunza Mtoto' meaning 'Care for the Child'. This programme was aimed at using health promotion as a way for people to take responsibility for their own health, in an area where there was little opportunity for medical care, with 68 per cent of children under five years of age in the first stage of malnutrition. There was also a high rate of infant mortality. Tana River has the highest rate of vitamin deficiency in Kenya.

Tom recruited a team of 30 people with different skills such as nurses, water technicians and driver mechanics. Eight of the team were armed police reserve officers who were recruited to provide security for the staff as the area was designated as an "Operational Area" by the authorities. "Operational Area" means that the area was insecure because of bandits crossing from the nearby Somali border. The Kenya authorities imposed restriction on travel in the whole Tana River district. Travel from Bangale to Garissa was by armed convoy and curfew was imposed from 7 pm to 6 am, meaning travel at night time was not allowed.

Together, the team trained 200 community health workers who would be "doctors" in their own villages. 98 per cent of women give birth at home with the assistance of Traditional Birth Attendants (TBAs). Part of the programme was to improve the skills of over 500 TBAs. Access to clean water was a major part of the development and his team, over a period of nine years, helped 100 villages to dig their own shallow wells. One village dug five wells before they struck safe water.

When the programme came to its end, Tom returned to Ireland to take up the role of Assistant Director in the Spiritan Asylum Service Initiative (SPIRASI). This is a Spiritan organisation, for which Tom's experience in both the fields of education and health were invaluable. From the outset, SPIRASI has focused on the provision of educational and integration support for asylum seekers, refugees and other disadvantaged migrant groups. In more recent years, SPIRASI's work has expanded to include the provision of rehabilitative care for survivors of torture and the provision of primary healthcare information for recent arrivals in Ireland.

Tom now ministers in the Holy Spirit Parish, Kimmage Manor, Dublin.

Why read about Tom's life?

Reading about Tom's life is of interest both to those who know him, having heard him in the past recounting individual stories at family events or Masses, as well as others who will appreciate not only his wit but those stories imbued with a deeper sense of meaning.

In addition, readers will gain a sense of what it takes to dedicate a lifetime to God by working as a missionary priest, and in doing so, not always taking the easiest option, but going where one is needed.

This is an extraordinary story of bravery under conditions that were sometimes adverse and dangerous. Yet he thinks of himself as a very ordinary person. However, despite the difficulties, Tom's humour shines through. He and others like him are the unsung heroes of our time. They can be found all over this world and their story deserves to be told.

Throughout his years in Africa, Tom has listened carefully to the stories of his elders and has made a most useful record of very interesting stories which otherwise would have been lost to posterity.

Furthermore, with the rapid decline in vocations to the priesthood evident in Ireland and many other countries in recent years, accompanied by a renewal of interest in volunteering within Ireland, it seems timely to write such a collection and offer a new challenge to us.

Tamsin Hogan

Map of Kenya

Part 1

MWATATE, TAITA, KENYA
1974 to 1982

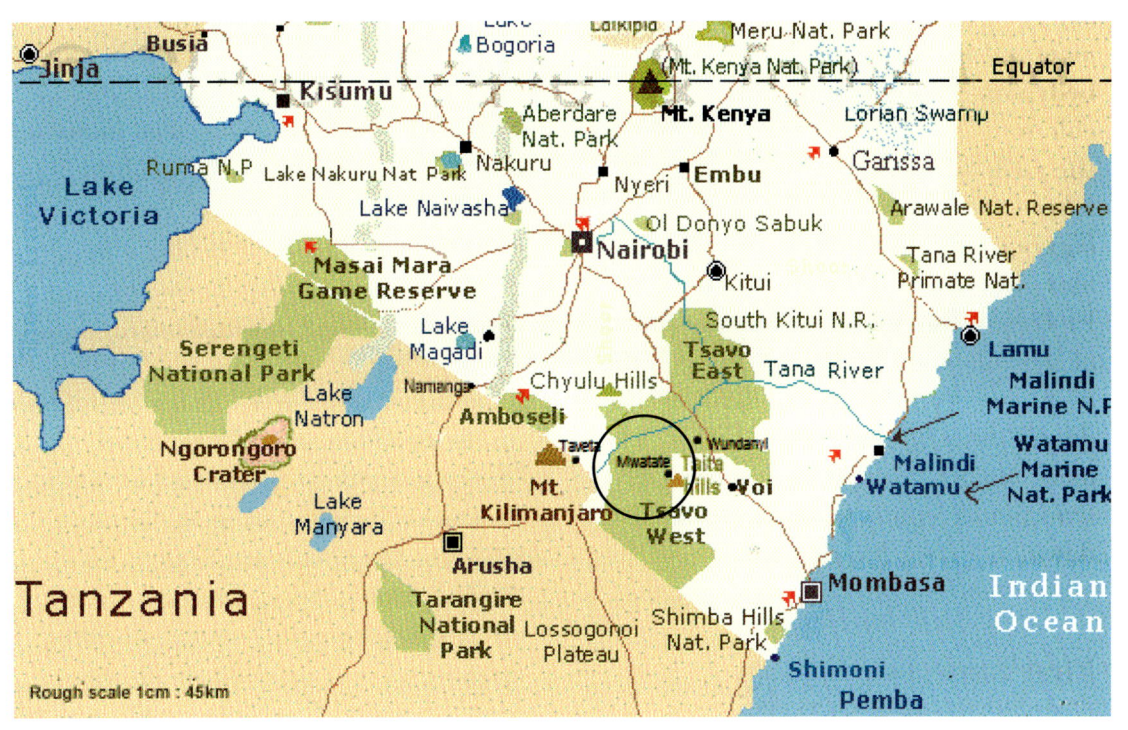

Introduction

I arrived in Kenya in September 1974 on a Sudan Airways flight, the cheapest airline on the route to East Africa. We landed for a refuelling stop and watched with wonder the sand dunes and rocks in the moonlight at Cairo airport. As we stepped out of the plane, we were met with a wall of heat.

On arrival in Kenya, I made my way to Mombasa. For the first two weeks, I stayed with my friend Fr Diarmuid Casey at Giriama mission, some miles outside the coastal town of Mombasa. My first nights in Africa were memorable. On being shown into my bedroom, I spotted a brightly coloured, good sized lizard clinging to the wall. *"This is a mosquito, but where you're going they are even bigger, so be sure to tuck in your mosquito net under the mattress."* Fr Paddy Roe joked. It was the time of the full moon and right through the night, you could hear the throb of the drums down in the nearby valley. The local Giriama people were having a traditional dance, which lasted until dawn.

First Funeral

At that time, a retired priest, Fr Jack Horber, was living with Diarmuid. Jack was from Switzerland and had been a pioneer missionary in Kenya. He was well looked after by his country in his retirement and a reasonable pension was paid to him by the Swiss government. Each year, Jack would have a visit from the Embassy and his pension would continue. Diarmuid always felt that they were coming to see if he was still alive! During my stay, the 90 year-old padre was suddenly taken ill, brought to hospital and called to his reward. I was asked to help with the funeral arrangements. Would I go into Mombasa town, purchase a coffin, receive the body from the mortuary and return to the mission?

I left in a battered Nissan pick-up truck and just about managed to find my way to Mombasa Cathedral. Arrangements were made to show me where to collect the coffin, the body and a large wooden cross. I went to "Resurrection Coffin Makers". Outside the workshop the sign board read "Resurrection Coffin Makers. Satisfaction is guaranteed. All customers will be looked after. No dissatisfied customers have ever returned to lodge a complaint."

I was directed to drive about 30 miles up the road towards Nairobi. At Mariakani village, I was told to make sure to turn right and go to Giriama mission. There was some fear about the possibility of my missing the turn off at Mariakani and ending up 300 miles away in Nairobi! Joe Castelino, one of the local Christians, volunteered to show me the way and he made sure I was on the road to Mariakani and not the one to Tanzania.

En route, I saw two Europeans hitch-hiking on the road. It was very hot at that time of the day and I felt pity for them, stopped and offered them a lift as far as Mariakani petrol station, where they would have a better chance of getting a lift. As they began to heave their knapsacks into the back of the pick-up truck, one of them noticed my luggage. *"What are you carrying there?"* the young man asked. *"Oh, that's Fr Horber. I am just bringing him home for burial,"* I replied. The "would-be" passengers stood back aghast and the bags were quickly offloaded. My kind offer was politely refused and I proceeded on my way with Fr Horber's body, the coffin and the cross. I arrived safely in good time for lunch.

The Christmas Radio

Once I settled in my new home, I started to learn Kiswahili. I went to Mgange Nyika, high up in the Taita Hills. The parish house had the most wonderful view. It faced Mount Kilimanjaro in Tanzania. At certain times of the year, Kilimanjaro was covered in cloud; then suddenly it would reveal itself in all its glory.

My first Christmas in Kenya was spent with Fr Vinny Browne and we celebrated Midnight Mass in the church at Mgange Dabidha. Vinny had succeeded in acquiring a reasonable command of Kiswahili. We agreed that Vinny would be principal celebrant and head preacher, while I would concelebrate and be master of ceremonies.

The Mass began well and the members of the choir were in fine voice. The traditional drums were throbbing and 'kiyambas' shakers were being played vigorously to accompany the Christmas Carols. Vinny was making a big effort to speak in his best Kiswahili. However, he had only just learnt the language and seemingly his language skills were not good enough for one of the faithful standing at the back of the church. This man had already begun to celebrate Christmas and was quite drunk. He had his radio with him. So, he said to one and all – *"This European can't speak our language, so I'll see the Mass here in Taita but listen to it from Dar es Salaam."* He tuned the radio to Radio Tanzania, which at that very time, was broadcasting Midnight Mass from Zanzibar Cathedral. The man turned up the volume to full so that he could hear clearly. The preacher from Zanzibar was really fired up and was certainly doing better than Vinny. The disturbance continued at the back of the church for a short time until the parish elders intervened and confiscated the offending radio. Later on, a church court was instituted by the elders and they fined the man one goat for the disturbance caused and for embarrassing Fr Browne. I seem to remember that the goat got eaten by an enlarged court!

Mwatate Parish and hot, hot plates

In 1974, I was appointed to Mwatate Parish in the Taita Hills, Mombasa District, where I lived for seven years. I taught English and Religion in Kenyatta Secondary School. I also helped in the parish and at various times was the Father in charge.

The house, built by Fr Brian Eburn in 1973, was nearly complete. Brian, who was born and educated in Kenya, was the first white Kenyan whom I met. He chose to situate the Mission house at the foot of Bura Bluff. It proved to be a good decision. Our home faced the lake at Mwatate in the Sisal estate. It was an idyllic setting with a commanding view of the countryside below. Sitting on the veranda, on your left, you could see the Voi road as it snaked its way over Mwatunge hill. On your right, you could see the little village of Mwatate and the road leading to Bura-Taita and onwards to Tanzania. Straight ahead, you could clearly see the lake in the Sisal estate and in the distance, the lower Pare Mountains in Tanzania.

Mwatate parish is situated between Tsavo East and Tsavo West National Parks. I used to joke that we had more elephants than Christians in the parish! On reflection, that statement was probably true! Residents of Kenya could buy a yearly ticket for entry to all the National Parks. We availed of this ticket and I made many visits to Tsavo National Park. After a while, I got to know the roads and the game areas quite well. This knowledge was to prove useful to me later in St Mary's School.

Our cook was Mama Hope, which is a very good name for a cook! My brother in law, Paul Cassin and his sister Enid, came to visit us and Paul kindly offered to help in the kitchen.

He noticed that Mama Hope always served food on cold plates, so he reminded her that plates should always be "hot, hot, hot". The following day our fresh salad arrived all shrivelled up on hot plates. We had a laugh and Paul held his peace.

The WaTaita People

The WaTaita people live in the Taita Hills in the south of Kenya. Their lands reach the Tanzanian border. They are a quiet and friendly people who have had little interest in the politics of Kenya. Over the years, they have faced regular bouts of drought and occasional floods during the rainy season. The heavy rain sometimes made the roads impassable, especially where there was black cotton soil. This glutinous soil simply stuck to the wheels and the tyres gathered more and more soil until the wheel arches were full, thus making driving impossible. There you would stay until someone dragged you out.

The WaTaita are Bantu people who speak a language called Kitaita, of which I had a working knowledge. One time, during a visit to South Africa, I was surprised to hear my cousin, Jimmy Fitzsimons, speaking in fluent Zulu – suddenly I realised I could understand him! It turns out that Zulu, Kiswahili and Kitaita are all Bantu languages and have similar constructions.

During my time in Mwatate, I saw that the people were very interested in getting their children to school and were aware of the importance of education.

Refugees from Mozambique

I met refugees for the first time in Mwatate. These were Makonde people from Mozambique who had fled the war during the time of Fremilo. Little did I know that I was to spend most of my life working with people from different countries! The Makonde people had been evangelised by Portuguese missionaries. They were from the old school and the Makonde certainly knew their religion and could even sing the Latin Mass.

Fr Bob Farrelly from Dublin celebrated the Golden Jubilee of his ordination while living with us in retirement in Mwatate. He told me that those years were the happiest years of his life. The elders in the parish asked permission to sing the Mass in Latin for the occasion. Their children were surprised to hear their parents, who had no literacy skills, singing the whole Mass in a language that the young people could not understand.

One morning, Feliciano, one of our catechists, arrived on my doorstep to inform me that one of his tribe, Mama Rosa, had died by suicide. Rosa was the mother of eight children. I was surprised, as I had been given to understand that suicide was rare in Africa. The burial ceremony took place after Mass in the Church. The Makonde people were desolate. When we had filled in the grave, the men of the tribe stamped their feet and through the rising cloud of dust, I could feel the force of their anger.

The turkey which really was a rooster!

The Sisters of St Joseph, a local Congregation at Bura, was founded by Bishop Eugene Butler of Mombasa Diocese. They raised turkeys and sold them at Christmas time. Nearly all the turkeys had been spoken for and Fr Mick Malone, the self appointed agent of the Sisters, had only one left to sell. He remembered that Fr Tom Roche, a Kerryman, had ordered one but had not turned up to collect it, so when Mick got the opportunity to sell it, he did so. However, that very evening, he was surprised to hear from some parishioners who had travelled up to the weekly market in Wundanyi, that Tom Roche had told them that he intended visiting Bura on the following day to collect his turkey!

What was he to do? He had promised Tom a turkey and yet he had sold it! So he told his cook: *"Take the head and neck of our slaughtered turkey and sew it onto the body of that big cock that we have been fattening."* Sure enough, the very next morning, he heard in the distance the familiar sound of Tom's Volkswagen as he slowly wound his way down the steep twisty road from the top of the Taita Hills.

When Tom turned up, he received a great welcome and was invited for a cup of morning tea. Afterwards, the cook brought out the turkey all nicely parcelled in brown paper, with the head hanging out. Tom was pleased with his purchase and went off a happy man, knowing that he was all set for Christmas as he was hosting the various Fathers from the surrounding missions. Hadn't his friend Mick Malone slaughtered the bird for him and had even put it in a nice paper bag: *"To keep the dust off,"* as he said.

When Tom got back to his mission, he handed the Christmas turkey to his cook who took one look and told Tom what was really in the paper bag. Tom was not amused at the time, but later saw the funny side and forgave Mick for his trick.

The washing of the feet

I made some progress in learning Kiswahili by Easter time – my first in Africa. Sisal, which is used to make ropes and seating, is grown in huge plantations in the area around Mwatate. We held the Holy Thursday ceremonies in the church situated in the Sisal estate. Linguistically, it was a challenge but I would be able to manage with the help of catechist Feliciano Mwendenao. Feliciano was a refugee from Mozambique. Together with his wife and children, he had fled the Frelimo conflict. He was to be my first close refugee contact.

We prepared for the Holy Thursday ceremony to be held at the Church and the faithful arrived. During this ceremony, twelve members of the congregation have their feet washed by the priest, in memory of the example given by Jesus when he washed his disciple's feet.

Twelve of the congregation were chosen and they were to sit on a bench in front of the altar and have their feet washed. I was to start washing the feet of the people at one end of the bench and then continue up the line. It was all very straightforward – or so I thought!

The back breaking work of cutting sisal was over for the day, people came from the camps all around the sisal estate for the ceremony which was held in the late afternoon. The church was packed and the ceremony began. It was going well enough and I had finished my homily. It was time to do the washing of the feet. I got the water, towel and basin from the altar boys who were helping in the ceremony. I started from the left, knelt down and began washing and then drying the feet of the chosen people. I was nearly finished my duties when I noticed that I seemed to have forgotten one or two who were still sitting at the other end of the bench. I returned and washed and dried the feet of the forgotten. Suddenly the bench was full again! Maybe I had misunderstood and twenty four people had been selected? Perhaps it was twelve men and twelve women; anyway I continued. Nevertheless, there were more and more people coming forward. I knew I was in for a long evening when I heard Feliciano saying: *"Father Tom is washing everyone's feet – this is a very big blessing, come forward row-by-row and be sure to bring all the children."*

Row-by-row they came, adults and children. By this time, the water was nicely coloured with the red dust of the area. The towel too became a bright coloured red. Maybe using a snow white towel wasn't such a good idea after all! So, every one had their feet washed, except myself. All were blessed. It was long ceremony but the people did not mind and felt that they had made a good start to the Easter festivities.

The man who rose from the dead

One day, the Christian leaders came to inform me that a body had been found just beside the Catholic Church in the sisal plantation. This was a serious incident and I suggested we report it to the local chief and the police. The body could not be identified as the hyenas and other wild animals had been feasting on it for some days. The police asked us to bury the body and so we prepared a deep grave in the ground near the church.

Curious spectators turned up to see what all the excitement was about. Suddenly, one of the many onlookers shrieked that this was the body of her missing husband! She recognised the decorated beaded Masai belt around the waist. That was the end of the funeral service for the time being. Now, the woman was a member of the Luo tribe and her husband would have to be buried according to their customs – relatives would have to be called, a wake and funeral ceremonies would have to be held and animals slaughtered and eaten, of course. We sympathised with her and the Church helped her financially with her husband's mourning ceremonies.

However, three months later, a man got off the bus from Taveta. There was consternation and many people were frightened – a 'dead' man had arrived into the village. Hadn't they been present when he was buried and wasn't his grave visible for all to see? As he walked towards people, they would step away from him. He was glad to be back home in the village but on alighting from the bus he was surprised when his friend frowned at him and walked away. He wondered what had he done so wrong? *"I have paid most of my niece's school fees"* he thought.

Eventually, someone came forward and told him that they had attended his burial! He was surprised to hear that and explained that he was not a ghost and he told his story. He had been given money to pay for his niece's school fees in Taveta High School, which was situated near the Tanzanian border. He set off in good time for the journey but as luck would have it, the bus broke down on the way, fortunately near Maktau village, where the weary travellers could get some food and drink. The day had been hot and he felt thirsty. He fell among bad company and went on a drinking and gambling spree. When all had been drunk or lost in a card game, he was dealt a great hand in the card game. He had nothing left to bet but his watch and his wonderful beaded leather belt. He knew he could not lose. He played his last card and to his amazement… he lost. Realising that the school fees were gone, he was too ashamed to return home. However, he still had the bus ticket to Taveta and the bus had been repaired, so on he travelled and got a labouring job on the sisal plantation at Taveta. When he had saved sufficient money, he paid some of the school fees and returned home to Mwatate repentant.

Everyone was astonished at the turn of events. He went home to his shack and his wife was overjoyed to see him. Being the good woman that she was, she came and thanked us for helping her bury her husband but he was now back in the land of the living! She wanted to return the money we had given her. *"Not at all, mother,"* we replied, *"the son who had been lost was now found. It's time for a celebration of life."* To this day he is known as "Ufukuko", meaning 'risen from the dead'.

But just who had we buried in the plot beside the church? Probably we will never know. But this much we do know – he took part in a card game in a "sheebeen" along the Taveta Road… and he had a winning hand!

Measles outbreak

In 1974, I had just begun teaching in Kenyatta High School and was also in charge of Mwatate parish. I was asked to a do quite a number of funerals for children and I was surprised by their increasing frequency. It was a time of great drought and there was a lot of malnutrition in the area. In fact, as the number of funerals increased, particularly children's funerals, I had to give up doing children's funerals as I had a full-time teaching post. We discussed the matter with the elders and it was decided that the catechists would have to do those services. I was to look after the living rather than the dead!

I realised that many of the children were dying of measles. This surprised me. I made various enquiries and found that the local cure for measles was to wrap the children in blankets and put them in the sun. I went to the local hospital and discovered that there was a disagreement among two hospitals as to which one was responsible for immunisation in the Mwatate area. I managed to get the matter clarified. I spoke in church and urged people to get their children immunised. We explained to them that cooking the children in the sun would not help them at that time, but that they should give the children lots of liquids and keep them in the shade to prevent dehydration. The people listened carefully to this sermon.

Nurses from the local Wesu hospital arranged to come and immunize the children in the local primary schools. The nurses from Wesu hospital arrived, dressed in their lovely white uniforms and walked up to the local primary school. As they entered the door of the classrooms... the children left by the windows! It was then that I learned that there was a belief that immunisation caused infertility. Somehow, we convinced the pupils to return to school and got them immunised.

A charitable journey and a bottle of whiskey

One November, during the time for the long rains, roads became impassable because of the thick glutinous mud. The road up and around the Taita hills was blocked on both sides of the hills by two landslides.

At the top of the hills, my friend Fr Jack Ryan was locked into his parish area for three weeks, but he was able to use his Volkswagen vehicle and go to Mgange Dabida church and two outstations at the top of the Taita hills. He was also able to visit the sick, as was his custom.

Each week, Jack would drive as far as he could and his cook would climb over the landslide and do the weekly shopping in nearby Wundanyi town. Sometimes, he also returned with twenty litres of petrol to fuel Jack's car. As I was the group leader in the Taita Hills at that time, I decided that I should pay him a visit.

One Friday, immediately after school, I drove up as far as the Chief's Office in Bura and left my car there and prepared to walk up the hills. I had packed a small knapsack with some useful items that might help Jack in his difficult situation. Among the packets of soups and a few tins of vegetables, I had a half bottle of Irish whiskey.

I walked up and over the landslides. It began to rain again and the going got tougher. Unfortunately, the inevitable happened and at one point, I fell down and broke the neck of the bottle of whiskey. I was very disappointed.

On arrival, I handed over my gifts and said: *"Jack I'm sorry but I broke the neck of the whiskey bottle when I fell down in the mud and rock."* Jack replied: *"Don't worry Tom, now you will know what a tea strainer is for"*, and he proceeded to decant the whiskey from the broken bottle through the strainer into a jug. It was a cold night at 6,000 ft altitude, despite the fire. The rains pounded down on the iron sheet roof and the wind whistled down the chimney and water came down the chimney too. Eventually, the fire was out and the hearth was filled with water. However, the whiskey helped to keep away the cold and of course we were forced to finish it, as the bottle had been damaged!

It was a good night and Jack played me a tune or two on his fiddle, while I sang "The Jug of Punch" and recited as many verses of Robert Service's poem "The Cremation of Sam McGee" as I could remember. I was glad I had made the journey, as I was his only visitor that month.

The power of Holy Water!

There is a little village called 'Mili Kumi' situated beside the edge of the railway track, just 10 miles from Voi on the way to Taveta, near the Tanzanian border. Mili Kumi, meaning "ten miles" was literally ten miles up the road from Voi to Taveta. The tiny sleepy village is the base camp for the rail gang who looked after a portion of the rail track. The rail was built as a spur or branch line during the First World War, to enable Allied troops move quickly to the Tanzanian Border where they faced the German-led 'Askari' troops of Tanganyika under the command of Lieutenant Colonel Von Lettow Vorbeck.

Otieno, who was a member of the gang looking after the railway line, came to see me. He reported that strange things were happening in his shack at night. His elder brother had died, leaving a wife and three children. In accordance with Luo custom, Otieno had inherited his brother's wife and children and was caring for them. Now his brother's spirit would visit him at night time to see how Otieno was getting on with his new wife and children!

The people asked me to perform an exorcism of the house. I knew that I did not have permission to perform such a ceremony as only certain priests within a Diocese are allowed to do an exorcism. I did not fancy doing it anyway. However, I said I would celebrate a mass at the shack and bless the home. I went there one evening with the other local Christians and we celebrated mass and I blessed the shack with lots of Holy Water. After that, the dead brother did not bother our man again. It just shows you the power of Holy Water!

Dembwa Catholic Church

With the arrival of priests living among the people on a permanent basis, the newly established parish began to expand. We identified a lovely site on Dembwa hill, looking out down the valley towards the Lower Pare Mountains in Tanzania.

The plan was to build a small church there. For two years, we celebrated Mass under the shade of a leafy tree beside the little river. It was during this time that we made the blocks for building a church. A German youth group joined with our Mwatate youth group in making the blocks for the building. We were surprised at lunch to see that our visitors would not eat the food provided for all. We enquired if something was wrong? They told us that they had seen the women drawing the water from the river and they thought that it could be contaminated. So the following day we said: *"We are going to bring water from the supply in the village."* It was the very same water, as the little river supplied the whole village! Then they began to eat the food, none the wiser. They ate every scrap.

We jokingly marked the cement blocks RC for Roman Catholic and called them Ronald Charo; this was because the local Anglican Church was also making blocks in the same area and we did not want any confusion. When all the blocks had been made, we now faced the difficulty of getting them up the hill. So we decided to start celebrating Mass up at the building site. Each Sunday, the adults would pick up a cement block and carry it up to the top of the hill for Mass. This block would be their seat for the morning. Children came with bags of small stones for ballast, which they brought up at the offertory and poured their offering into large tin cans called 'debes'. After Mass, the elders would carefully put all the cement blocks aside so that on the next Sunday, more blocks would have to be carried. After a year, all the blocks were on site and we never had to buy any ballast for the foundations, as the children had supplied enough from their 'debes'.

Fr Frank Caffrey designed and supervised the building and put coloured glass in the cross-shaped window behind the altar. And in the evening time, you could see the fading sunlight shining through this window as you drove up the steep, switchback road to Wundanyi. My godmother, Freda Cullinane, funded an altar in memory of her husband Anthony Cullinane, who was my godfather. Frank managed to find a very beautiful altar made by a Sikh artisan from Mombasa. We installed it one Sunday and put a little plaque there in memory of Freda and Anthony.

Mama Helena

For many years, Mama Helena was the chairlady of Dembwa Catholic Church. She had a number of children and her eldest son came and told me that he wanted to be a priest. He was a good living young man, in sound health and with sufficient ability for the long studies required for priesthood. He seemed a suitable candidate to us. I went to Mama Helena and her son explained that he wanted to become a priest. Mama Helena refused, saying that the youngest could become a priest but not the eldest. In the local tradition, the eldest son is expected to be the breadwinner, marry and have children. Time passed by and the young boy grew up troublesome.

Some years later, I heard that there was no priest for Mwatate Parish. Mama Helena had gone with the elders to see Nicodemus Kirima, the Archbishop of Mombasa Diocese. They complained that they had no priest to look after them. *"I'm sorry but we do not have any priests available at this time"*, the Archbishop told them. However, if she had allowed her eldest son to be a priest, events might have been different!

The sleeping lion

My young nephew, Stephane Hogan, was staying in Kenya with us during his summer holidays from school. His parents decided that Africa might be a good place for a 16-year-old to learn about life. Stephane got a learner's driving licence and I taught him to drive. Frank Caffrey and I decided we should travel with him and some friends to the Masai Mara Game Reserve to see the wild animals. As there were only seats in the pick-up truck for three, my nephew and I would have to stay in the back of the truck. We prepared the vehicle and welded a mesh wire to the metal frame at the back of the vehicle. This hopefully would protect us from wild animals when we were in the game reserve. We cut two holes in the wire mesh so that Stephane and I would be able to sit up on the roof of the truck and have a very good view of all the animals. We put some canvas as a back door at the rear of the vehicle. It gave the impression of safety with all the wild animals around. Off we went on our journey to the Masai Mara Game Reserve. It was a dirt road and very dusty – so much so that my nephew and I got into our sleeping bags to escape from the fine dust, but it was of no use. The dust penetrated everywhere.

Stephane asked Frank, who was driving, to stop so that he could *"bless the land"*, as he said. He got down from his perch on the roof and was about to climb down from the back of the truck when he noticed a lion by the side of the road. *"There's a dead lion here"*, he said just as he stepped down. No sooner had his foot touched the ground, than the dead lion opened one eye!! Stephane leaped back into the truck and could not go to the toilet for hours! We all had a good laugh.

Always turn left

My mother came to live with us in Kenya a number of times. She would avoid the harsh Irish winter weather and stay for some months in Kenya, before going down to South Africa to visit my sister Helena. This gave my family a good excuse to travel and escort her down to South Africa. I managed to obtain a special re-entry visa on two occasions to enable me to travel to South Africa. I was fortunate that my Headmaster, Sammy Maneno, had shared a room with the Chief Immigration Officer, when they were mature students in university. Sammy gave me a good letter of introduction to the officer and I got my visa.

During my mother's time with us, she helped many children who were suffering from eye infections. At first, she used to give the mothers tubes of antibiotic ointment to be used to cure the infection. However, she soon discovered that the ointment was not being applied correctly. With the shortage of water, hygienic conditions were difficult to maintain. Children with one infected eye were returning with both eyes infected. She decided that the mothers would have to bring the babies to her daily. She would administer the medicine herself. Those mothers who came regularly had their babies' eye infections cured. Those who didn't ended up with blind adolescents.

'Mama Tom', as my mother was called, learned to drive the Chevrolet pick-up truck and on a number of occasions would drive sick patients to

Voi hospital. On one occasion, we were called to go and see a sick girl in a nearby village which was full of women and children; there were no men around that afternoon. We had one look at the sick girl and saw that she was unconscious. We recommended immediate hospitalisation. But the women told us that they were unable to come to a decision by themselves. They would have to wait for the village elders to return. I reminded them that the government exams were to start on the following day and that I was the chief supervisor. I would not be able to return and pick up the girl. It was now or never. Nevertheless, they could not come to a decision.

Sure enough, bright and early on the following morning, the elders were on my doorstep. I explained that as I had to start the government exams at a set time, I would not be able to help with the transport of the sick girl. They asked me if there was any way that I could help. I thought about my mother. Would she be able to drive the Chevrolet pick-up truck across the dry river bed and climb up the steep bank on the opposite side? I asked her if she was prepared to try. I offered for catechist Vitalis to be her guide. I always liked his name – it was a well know brand of hair lotion at the time! Vitalis knew some English – at least that is what I thought! Mama Tom agreed and got into the driving seat. Then the elders approached me and asked quietly: *"Does this old Mama really know how to drive?"* I reassured them and all twelve piled into the vehicle and were off.

As Mama Tom proceeded on her journey, at each and every junction Vitalis would say, "Next turn left". It did not seem to matter if it was a left or right turn! It was always "Next turn left" even when there was no road! After a few hiccups, Mother eventually found herself facing a dry riverbed with a steep bank on the far side. She muttered something about the Irish rally driver, Rosemary Smith. She engaged first gear and put her foot to the floor. The car just flew down the bank, across the riverbed and straight up the far side. Afterwards she told us: *"She who hesitates is lost"*. There were no more comments from the elders on her driving ability!

Oral Literature; the monkey and the turtle

When I was teaching in Kenyatta High School, Taita, in Kenya, I began to become aware of oral literature and its great wealth. The African people are great storytellers and have a wonderful facility for remembering their traditional stories. Together with students, we explored those traditional stories. And here is an adaptation of some of the stories, which I have written up for my grand-nephew, Tom Behrens, who lives in Melbourne, Australia.

You have asked me for a story – are you ready for a long one? Are you all sitting comfortably? Then, let us begin.

In the biggest jungle of Africa, a troop of monkeys lived and Jumatatu, the strongest, was their leader. However, as the years passed, Jumatatu became old, grey and weak. One day, the young monkeys in the troop decided it was time to change their leader.

When Jumatatu came down from his tree for the usual monthly meeting, the young monkeys were waiting for him. They suddenly all attacked him and he couldn't fight back because he had become old. After a short fight, he went back to the top of the tree to rest. Yet, the other young monkeys wouldn't let him rest. They continued to fight. He knew he could not fight back so he decided to run away from his troop. He went far away from them and found a new homeland which he called Wenje and it was full of mango trees, beside the beautiful Tana River.

Drawing of 'The Monkey and the Turtle' by Tom's niece, Sarah Lawler

One day, Jumatatu was so bored from being alone all the time, he was scratching himself as he had no one else to scratch, for as you know, monkeys like to scratch each other every day. He was really bored and he decided to throw some of the mangoes into the river to see what would happen. A turtle was swimming nearby and he thought that the monkey had seen him and had given him the mangoes. Another day, the turtle came back and again there were some delicious mangoes in the water. This time, the turtle poked his head out of the water, licked his big lips and thanked Jumatatu for the present. Now, Jumatatu didn't know why he was being thanked, but he said: *"Ok Mr Turtle, no problem."* And the turtle, on impulse, asked the monkey to become his friend and Jumatatu accepted. Over the next while, they became very good friends indeed.

One day, a neighbour called to Mr Turtle's house and asked his wife: *"Where is Mr Turtle?"* She replied: *"My husband has become friends with a monkey. He now spends all of his time with this new friend and now he hardly ever comes home at all."*

The neighbour replied: *"It's not good for you at all. You should think of something to bring your husband home again."* Mrs Turtle said: *"Please tell me how I can bring my husband back home."*

The neighbour thought and thought, and then he thought and thought again and he frowned a lot. Very many lines appeared on his forehead, steam came out of his ears because of all his thinking and then after a short time he suggested: *"Pretend to be ill and when your husband comes back, I'll tell him you're very, very sick. I will also tell him that we went to your doctor and that you must eat a monkey's heart, to be cured from your sicknesses."*

Mrs Turtle said: *"This is a clever plan. Let us try it when he comes back home."*

Sure enough, after a few days, Mr Turtle returned and Mrs Turtle spotted him and quickly hid under a blanket. Mr Turtle went inside his house and called and called for his wife. Then his neighbour turned up and said to him: *"What is all the noise about? Oh, Mr Turtle, it is yourself, welcome back."* After thanking his neighbour, Mr. Turtle said: *"Where is my wife?"*

"Oh your wife – yes your wife was very ill and I brought her to hospital. The doctor said she can only get better when she eats a monkey's heart – a real live monkey's heart." He paused a little and then said: *"You have a monkey friend, don't you?" "Yes,"* replied Mr Turtle, *"my good friend the monkey is called Jumatatu". "Well, go and tell him to give you his heart and bring it to your wife so she'll become better,"* said the neighbour.

Now Mr Turtle went straight back to his friend Jumatatu and all the way he was thinking about his problem. What could he say to trick Jumatatu to go to his home? So he said: *"My loving wife, Mrs Turtle, wants to meet you and she has invited us both to our house. She has cooked a big chicken and wants to feed us very well."*

Jumatatu agreed and off they went, Jumatatu swinging from tree to tree and Mr Turtle slowly plodding along, for as you know, turtles cannot walk very quickly, they just waddle along. However, they soon came to the wide river and the trees were too far apart for Jumatatu to swing from and as you know, monkeys cannot swim very well. Then Mr Turtle said: *"Jumatatu, jump on my back, I can swim very, very well and I will carry you across."* And he started to swim across. In the middle of the river, the turtle began to think about how he was betraying his good friend. He felt very sad and he stopped swimming and slowly, slowly the turtle began to sink under the weight of Jumatatu. The water began to touch Jumatatu's tail and he grew frightened. *"What is wrong Mr Turtle?"*, Jumatatu asked, *"We are sinking".*

"Listen, my friend Jumatatu, I have lied to you. My wife did not invite you at all. She is very ill and the doctor told her she has to eat a monkey's heart in order to get better. You're my friend and I don't want to lie to you. I want to take you home and ask you for your heart," the turtle said.

Thinking very quickly, Jumatatu said: *"Oh my dear friend, why did you not tell me before?"*

"Why?" asked the turtle.

"You see we monkeys never take our hearts with us when we go to a friend's house and I have left mine at home at the top of a mango tree." So they agreed to go back to Jumatatu's home in Wenje and collect his heart.

When Mr Turtle swam close to the mango trees Jumatatu quickly jumped up into the trees. And he climbed and climbed until he reached the very, very top. Mr Turtle waited and waited for Jumatatu but he was nowhere to be seen. Finally, Mr Turtle called out and Jumatatu answered: *"Go home my friend. I don't want to give you my heart to take to your wife. You have betrayed me and now I don't want to see you anymore."*

"You are so right. I am so sorry about what I did," said Mr Turtle. "I shouldn't have done it. Please forgive me. I promise you it will never happen again."

Jumatatu thought about this and finally said: *"Ok, I will try to forgive you and only time will tell what kind of friend you really are."*

The turtle returned to his sick wife. He told his wife all about Jumatatu the monkey, and that he had lied to Jumatatu and how the monkey had even forgiven him, even though he knew that Mr Turtle and the neighbour had planned to take out his heart. Mrs Turtle felt very sorry for her husband and told how she too had lied about being sick. Then Mr. Turtle forgave his wife and over time Mr. Turtle and the monkey became friends again.

And a long, long time later, Mrs Turtle did indeed cook a large chicken for them. Jumatatu brought a lot of juicy mangoes and they made a lovely stuffing. The chicken was so big that it looked like a turkey! They all ate very well and had a wonderful time. And so all of them learned that it is better to forgive and forget, rather than being bitter and sad all the time.

Birth stories

I was invigilating the Kenyan National Examinations at Voi Secondary School which had been founded by my predecessor Fr Sean O'Connell.

Just before setting off one morning, I learned that Marylene, the wife of my catechist Venant, was having trouble in childbirth. I rushed over and told the midwife that we would have to leave for the hospital without delay, as the Government exam had to start on time. Without any fuss, Venant piled his wife and the midwife into the car and we set off at top speed. We made very good time because as Marylene's contractions came more frequently, I seemed to drive faster!

Later on that day, Marylene gave birth to a healthy baby boy. The doctor told her that whoever had got her to the hospital in time had saved the baby's life and in recognition of my efforts, the baby was called after me. This beautiful black baby was given the name of 'Thomas Hogan Mjomba'. Later on, he became a policeman and was promoted through the ranks. Hopefully, one day I will meet him again.

Some time later, I was called to the sub-chief's house. His 17 year-old daughter was having trouble giving birth to her first child. The traditional birth attendant told me that the girl would have to be taken to hospital as the contractions has been going on for hours and the girl was simply exhausted.

She was carried to the car and various helpers climbed into the Fiat 124. There were six of us. How there was room for the pregnant woman as well, I don't know! The girl was crying out as we flew along. The more she cried for her mother, the faster I drove. I remember hitting 130 kms at one stage on the tarmac section. The car had never gone so fast! The people encouraged the screaming girl *"Now you will love your mother!"* they shouted. We arrived at the hospital in a cloud of dust. I ran and called a nurse who came to the car with a delivery kit. She quickly saw that the girl had already given birth and that the child had been strangled by the umbilical cord. The grandmother said *"Shauri ya Mungu"* (It is in God's hands). The nurse replied *"No, Granny, it's your fault. Why did you not stop the European on the journey?"* But the grandmother said that she was too frightened to tell the European to stop. I was so angry when I heard her answer but held my peace.

The curious case of the woman in the mirror

Every year, Nesphor Righa came to stay with me during the holidays from his studies at the seminary. Eventually, he was ordained with great celebration up in Mgange Nyika at the top of the Taita Hills. Soon after, he was appointed to the Kenyan Navy as a chaplain and after his course, he was commissioned as an officer. He looked wonderful in his brilliant white uniform.

Once, he asked me if I could help him in moving a new wardrobe to his family home where he had built a room for himself. During that time, I had the loan of a large Volkswagen Combi van and so it was not difficult to transport the wardrobe to its new home up in the hills. Mama Righa helped me unload the wardrobe and we put it into the room. She admired the lovely wooden door and opened it to see the inside. Then, very quietly, she asked me: *"Fada Tom, why does my son have a picture of a woman in his big box?"* I then explained that the woman standing in the mirror of the big box was her own reflection! She was amazed and said that she had never seen anything like that. We had a laugh and I told her that we had a similar story from the West of Ireland.

Some years later Nesphor was found murdered in the Kenya naval base at Mombasa. I attended his funeral which was a very sad occasion.

The ambulance that became a meat van

The need for an ambulance was often expressed by the community. Our pick-up truck was not really suitable for transporting sick people. We knew Brian Burrows, who was the manager of the nearby Taita Hills, Salt Lick Hilton Hotel. He was a "larger than life" character who appears in Robert Ruarks book "Uhuru" as the manager of the Norfolk Hotel, which in fact he once had been. He used to call into our house occasionally for 'real food'. He used to say that he was fed up with hotel type food and wanted the simple fare that happened to be on our table that evening.

Frank Caffrey, who was now the Parish Priest, suggested raising the money for the ambulance project by entertaining tourists with music at the hotel. Brian liked the idea and said it would give the tourists an opportunity to meet some local young people.

Dressed up in colourful African cloth, a group of young ladies used to accompany me on the guitar, singing religious Swahili music and playing the drums. Eventually, they even learned to sing a few songs in German so that they could impress the visitors.

Eventually, assisted by donations, we raised the money for a pick-up truck with a specially made body to serve as the local ambulance. It took some time to source the vehicle, as we had to wait for it to come from Japan. I had just been transferred before the ambulance arrived and Frank Caffrey was then asked to transfer to St Mary's School in Nairobi and join me there. Unfortunately, the new parish priest did not want to be seen driving around in an ambulance and wanted a saloon car. So the brand new ambulance was returned to the Cathedral compound and a second-hand car purchased for the parish instead. We were surprised to hear, some time later, that the ambulance was being used for delivering meat! The people were very disappointed. This was a far cry from its intended function. Such problems are familiar to those involved in development work, whereby people managing projects are transferred to new pastures and new people take over the project with their own ideas and different forces come into play.

New names for us: 'Wakio and Mwangeka'

Before I left Mwatate, I was made a member of the Taita tribe and given the name 'Mwangeka'. Now Mwangeka had been a tribal leader, who had galvanised the Taita people and led them to resist the Masai warriors who used to raid the area in search of cattle and women – in that order. This was quite an honour, as very few of our priests had been given this recognition by the Wataita.

My mother also was made a member of the tribe and given the name "Wakio" meaning "born in the morning". She was given this name because of the health work that she had accomplished

Mwatate – Looking out over our church towards Voi

Mwatate – The magnificent view from our verandah facing the Pare Mountains in Tanzania

My mother, 'Mama Tom' comes on one of her regular visits

Some young parishoners come to have their picture taken beside the bouganvillia

Our Christmas Choir Group singing in the Salt Lick Hilton Lodge

*A fundraising event to enable us to finish the church.
You can just see 'Mama Tom' jitterbugging behind me!*

Teacher Vincent receives a donation from 'Mama Tom', with Fr. Frank Caffrey looking on

Mwatate – Traditional dancing in Church

A church celebration in the Sisal Estate to welcome my sister Maureen and our sister-in-law, Oonagh

Our pick-up truck is stuck on a hill on the way to our quarry

Volunteer, Steven O'Rafferty, leads from the front in recovering our pick-up truck

All aboard! – our pick-up truck doubles as a bus!

Our singing group performs with Fr. Tom in Salt Lick Hilton Lodge

Ladies of the parish preparing food on our verandah for a church function

We visit a Masai Manyatta

Students of Kenyatta High School and Fr. Tom in an outdoor performance of Joe de Graft's play, 'Muntu'

Our nursery school teacher, Maria, and friends come to visit

while she was with us. The only other woman, that I know of, who had been given this honour was Miss Murray, an Anglican missionary who had started a girls' school in the Taita Hills, later to be named in her honour.

The naming ceremony took place early one Sunday morning. Mother and I were dressed up in suitable regalia – myself with a wrap-around sheet called a "Shuka". A bow and arrow were given to me to protect the tribe. Mama Tom was dressed up for the occasion with clothing made from two "shukas". She was given the long Taita earrings and a bag for carrying the vegetables. The long strap of the bag would be hung from the forehead and the luggage carried on the back.

In 1982, Fr. Oliver Ellis, the district leader, arrived on visitation, during which he asked me to take up a position at St Mary's School in the Archdiocese of Nairobi. My mother was staying with me at the time and Ollie explained that he had two flats, side by side, which might prove a home for us. When I told her I had agreed to go to Nairobi, she said: *"I'll fly home tomorrow."* *"No please don't,"* I replied. *"There will be a place for you as well. We are both being transferred."* And so we set off in our little Toyota Corolla for St Mary's, wondering what the next few years would bring. Later on, when I was made Headmaster, she was very proud and made sure that I was dressed for the part!

Part 2

ST. MARY'S SCHOOL, NAIROBI
1982 to 1995

Introduction

St Mary's School had been opened in 1939, just before the outbreak of the Second World War. European settlers hesitated to send their children overseas for education, because they suspected that war would break out. They asked the Spiritans to start a boarding school for boys, since the Loreto Sisters had already built a school for the girls. At the beginning, the school started with thirteen European boys, but later on as it developed, the school opened its doors to children of every race and creed. When I was headmaster, the school enrolment reached 1,500 students.

St Mary's is situated in the grounds of St Austin's Mission. The mission was started on a large farm in 1889 by French Holy Ghost Fathers. It was here that coffee was first successfully grown in Kenya and for many years French Mission coffee seedlings were the only one's permitted for use in the Kenya colony. Karen Blixen, in her book, *Out of Africa*, mentions riding over on Sunday mornings to the mission to share a glass of red wine and speak French with the Fathers.

A private Catholic school, St Mary's caters for both primary and secondary education. Girls attend for the final two years. It offers both national and international curricula such as the General Certificate of Education, London (GCE's) and the International Baccalaureate.

The best in the world

In 1993, one of our pupils, Sneha Patel, achieved a perfect score in the International Baccalaureate and was placed first in the world. She was the only pupil to score a perfect mark that year.

Sneha was a very popular girl and was elected by pupils and teachers as one of the school leaders. She had taken a principal role in our musical *"Fiddler on the Roof"* in her year. She was a good example of the all-round education that we strove to give our pupils. Sneha was everyone's heroine when I gave the school a free day in honour of her achievement.

While this unique achievement received recognition in the national Kenya papers, it received no notice among the Spiritan publications, despite their having been given photos and a write-up of the event. There are few of our schools and fewer of our headmasters who can say that one of their students has come first in the world!

The International Baccalaureate programme incorporates two hours supervised social work weekly. As the number of pupils doing the International Baccalaureate programme increased, it was difficult to organise transportation for all students around the city for social work. A number of programmes were established to keep some of the pupils in the school for their social work. One was first-aid. I qualified as a first-aid trainer with St John's Ambulance organisation. Over the years, I trained over 200 pupils in first-aid. This skill was to prove very helpful to a number of my students.

Once, one of my pupils was a passenger in his father's car on a journey from Nairobi to Mombasa. It is a long drive so they started early and there was mist on the road. Unfortunately, they missed a sign stating "Diversion", and sped gaily on into a set of barrels filled with stones. My pupil was asleep in the back of the car and when the impact happened, he was unhurt. However, his parents were both injured and were bleeding profusely. He was able to staunch their bleeding, get them to Machakos hospital and make a phone call to the Flying Doctor. His parents were soon transported to a Nairobi hospital and were well cared for. Afterwards, I told his parents: *"You gave your son life, but he gave life back to you."*

St Mary's tries to bring out the best in every pupil. Every talent of any type is encouraged. There are a big variety of sports and clubs available to pupils - from first-aid to mechanics, from a cookery club to ornithology. Music was a big part of life in St Marys, which had a school orchestra, the only one in East Africa. I was able to help repair a number of instruments and acquire new ones. Each year, the school put on a musical which ranged from Gilbert and Sullivan's *"Pirates of Penzance"* to *"Oklahoma"* and *"My Fair Lady"* by Rodgers and Hammerstein. Each year, I would organise a "Mystery Tour" for the orchestra. This encouraged them to put in the long hours of practice necessary to master a musical instrument.

I lived and worked in the school for thirteen years. There were happy yet challenging times and each year was different in its own way. Initially, I was Dean of Form One's, then for six years was Principal of Primary and later on, Headmaster of the whole school for a further six years.

On becoming headmaster, I abolished corporal punishment. There had been a custom of using the leather strap on the primary boys and a bamboo cane on the secondary pupils. I had always felt uneasy about this. In addition, with encouragement and support from the staff, we set in place a new type of leadership. Staff and students were allowed a say in who would become student leaders.

One time, Viloo Nowrojee, one of our teachers, asked me for permission to go to South Africa to speak at a conference dealing with the rights of the child. I asked her to greet my Aunt Dorothy Cooper in Fishhoek, Cape Town. Sometime later, I was very pleased to hear that my Aunty Dot was telling everyone that Mrs Nowrojee had dedicated her talk at the conference to her headmaster, Father Tom Hogan, who had taken the brave decision to abolish corporal punishment in a 1,500 pupil school.

There are lots of stories about the early days of Saint Mary's. Fr Frank Soughley, who lived there for many years, was a great raconteur and told me some of them.

Rapture Road

There are a number of brothels in Nairobi and one is situated on Rapta Road, right beside the front gate of the school. One evening, the school bus broke down on Rapta Road in front of the brothel. The students thought it was very funny and renamed the road 'Rapture Road'. However, the headmaster at that time, Fr Paul Cunningham from Dublin, did not see the joke and was most anxious to move the bus that evening, even if it had to be dragged!

The octopus and its tentacles

There is a Carmelite Convent near St Mary's School. A group of priests from the school were chaplains to the convent, officiating at all the religious services there. On one occasion, one of our priests was giving them a spiritual talk. While intending to discuss the significance of the octopus and his tentacles, he actually enlightened the somewhat bewildered group of sisters on the "octopus and his many testicles". Whatever point this example was meant to illustrate, the sisters couldn't remember. All they could remember were the testicles of the octopus!

"Thank you for wasting your time"

It is said that many jokes are based on misunderstandings. I have come across a number, which involve language. We had many visitors in St Mary's as Nairobi airport is a large international hub. I heard many a story. Fr Tony Byrne, an Irish priest who had worked in Nigeria, visited us and told us when he first went to spend some time teaching in secondary schools, one of the pupils made a speech: "Thank you for coming here to waste your time teaching us."

The dead body

One of my friends, another Irish priest, was driving home from Nairobi one dark night. As he came around a bend, his headlights picked up the shape of something or someone lying in the middle of the road and he made an emergency stop. On investigation, he saw it was a man who had been knocked down and injured, but was still alive. He managed to drag the man over and put him into the Volkswagen car. He drove directly to the hospital, where he was surprised to be told that his passenger was already dead and that he should go to the police. This he did and the police told him that he should bring the body to the morgue. The people at the morgue told him that he should go back to the hospital and get a death certificate from the doctor. He went back to the hospital and was told that he would have to wait to get the certificate on the following morning.

So what was he to do? Remembering that no one had asked him his name and that the police had not written down the details of his car, he had the solution! He went to the outpatient department and sat the man in the chair so that he would be first in line the next morning and get immediate attention! Then the priest went home with an easy conscience, knowing full well that he had tried to help the "sick" man.

A serious case of worms

Fr Charlie Gabrione was an ex U.S. marine who had become a Spiritan. Frank Soughley told me that there was a story about Charlie and his cure for worms. I was interested in the story as soon as I heard its title – a cure for worms is very useful in Africa. It happened that some of the parishioners had a drinking problem in Charles Gabrione's parish in Tanzania. He decided that he should tackle the problem and preach against excessive alcohol consumption.

Charlie, as he was known, was a good preacher who always tried to illustrate his point with visual aids. One day, he brought a glass of the local whiskey and a live worm to the pulpit. He spoke on the danger of drinking and how too much alcohol consumption is bad for you. To strike his point home, he dropped the worm into the whiskey. All eyes were fixed on the glass and sure enough, after a short time the worm died. *"You see, this is what will happen to you!"* he said, and that was the end of his sermon, or so he thought! Some days later, he was surprised when he was thanked by some people in the marketplace for his new cure for worms – whiskey!

The message in a bottle

Some years ago, I was very interested to read an article in an Irish newspaper "The Munster Express" entitled *"The Extraordinary Story of the Message in a Bottle"*. A Waterford man explained that some years ago when he was a young 14 year-old boy, he wrote a message on a piece of paper, sealed it in a bottle and then threw it into the ocean at Tramore beach. He asked the finder of the bottle to send him a card.

A few days later, the young man was surprised when he received a postcard with a French postmark on it. It was from a young French girl called Patricia who had found the bottle while she was walking together with her uncle on Tramore beach. She brought it with her to the car ferry and then threw it into the English Channel on her way to France that very evening.

A few months later, the young man was more than delighted to receive another card. This time the card was from South Africa. A young boy named Kevin wrote to say that one day, as he was trawling for yellow-tail fish with his uncle 'Shummy' Russell, they spotted a bottle in the water on the Atlantic side of the Cape of Good Hope. They wrote to say that they had recovered the bottle and had brought it to the East Coast of the Cape and thrown it into the Indian Ocean and hoped that someday it would reach India.

Amazingly, the following Christmas, a third postcard arrived! This time it was from Kenya. Mark, a young student of St Mary's school, Nairobi, wrote to say that he had found a bottle while on a school trip studying the coral reef at Mombasa. Mark and his class mates had recovered the bottle and had got some fishermen to drop it far out to sea.

What really happened to the message in the bottle was this: One day as my niece Patricia and I were walking on Tramore beach, we found a bottle with a message inside. We opened it and noted the name and address and I said: *"We will brighten up this young boy's life!"* So my niece Patricia wrote the first card, while my nephew Kevin Behrens in South Africa wrote the second and Mark Muinde, a student of mine in Kenya was happy to write the third card.

Little did I suspect that years later, I would read of the matter in the newspaper and see a picture of a young man standing proudly with the three postcards in a picture frame? I read the story and suddenly realised that this was our doing! Truly it was the amazing story of the Message in a Bottle. I recently came across the young man's address. Perhaps it is time to send another postcard – maybe from Australia! Or maybe I should send one from Tramore where the bottle was originally thrown into the sea!

The great April fool's gag

It was the morning of April 1st and as usual the bell rang at 8.30 a.m. sharp for silence in St Mary's for the school assembly. I, as headmaster, went up the steps to the podium in the quadrangle to take the assembly. All the students, 1,450 of them, were lined up in their respective classes in front of me. Their class teachers were with them and other teachers were standing at the classroom corridors on three sides of the quadrangle. I had just greeted the students when suddenly a series of loud explosions rang out from one of the two water towers that overlooked the quadrangle. The noise was tremendous. Fortunately, I realised that the noise was not from gun shots and just said very cynically: *"Thank you very much"*, and everyone laughed. Now, it happened around that time that some civil unrest had taken place in the city. I had been forced to close the school on a number of occasions that year. If I had dived to the floor in front of the students, we could have had a dangerous stampede. Two of the teachers rushed up to the towers to see who had made the noise like gun fire, but all they found was burnt fireworks and a long, delayed-action fuse.

We had a quick meeting of senior teachers and resolved to solve the puzzle. On investigation, Mr George Joseph, our resident Sherlock Holmes, found one small primary boy who said that he had seen a tall European boy going up to the top of the tower a few minutes before the assembly. We had

Standard Seven students climb Mount Longonot in 1982, with Fr. Tom Hogan, Miss Josephine O'Hare and Mr. John Opot

Teacher Winnie Fernandes gets a helping hand from Alice

Fr. Tom with Cardinal Maurice Otunga, and his Excellency the Papal Nuncio on the occasion of St. Mary's Golden Jubilee

The Turkana bus crossing the Suguta River

Rugby is a very popular sport in St. Mary's

My Christian Religion Education class, Standard 8

Safari outfitters, Abercrombie and Kent, ask us to take part in a Bike Trek

Bike Trek on Masai cattle trails in the Kajiado area

Fr. Tom leads the Guest of Honour, Prof. Norah Olembo, through the Guard of Honour

A student plays the violin in the Prize Day concert

Parent and Guest of Honour, Prof. Norah Olembo, signs the Visitors' Book

The Moto Moto car rally and students with their hand-made cars

And they are off!

Headboy, Peter Angwenyi, with Fr. Tom and Guest of Honour, Prof. Olembo

Headgirl, Lillian Attere and Carol Ngori win the Victor Ludorum

School leaders, elected by the students and teachers, with Fr. Tom

Our Recorder Group play an item in the concert

Our International Baccalaureate students with their 'Ipi Tombi' Zulu dance for Prize Day concert

The magnificent setting for the Prize Day celebrations

Mr. Semu conducts the Junior Orchestra

An International Baccalaureate student demonstrates a science experiment

This is our Headmaster!

The Headmaster gives his Annual Report

All ready for Assembly in Saint's!

Fr. Tom Hogan on Prize Day

'The Government Inspector' by Nikili Gogol, directed by Fr. Tom

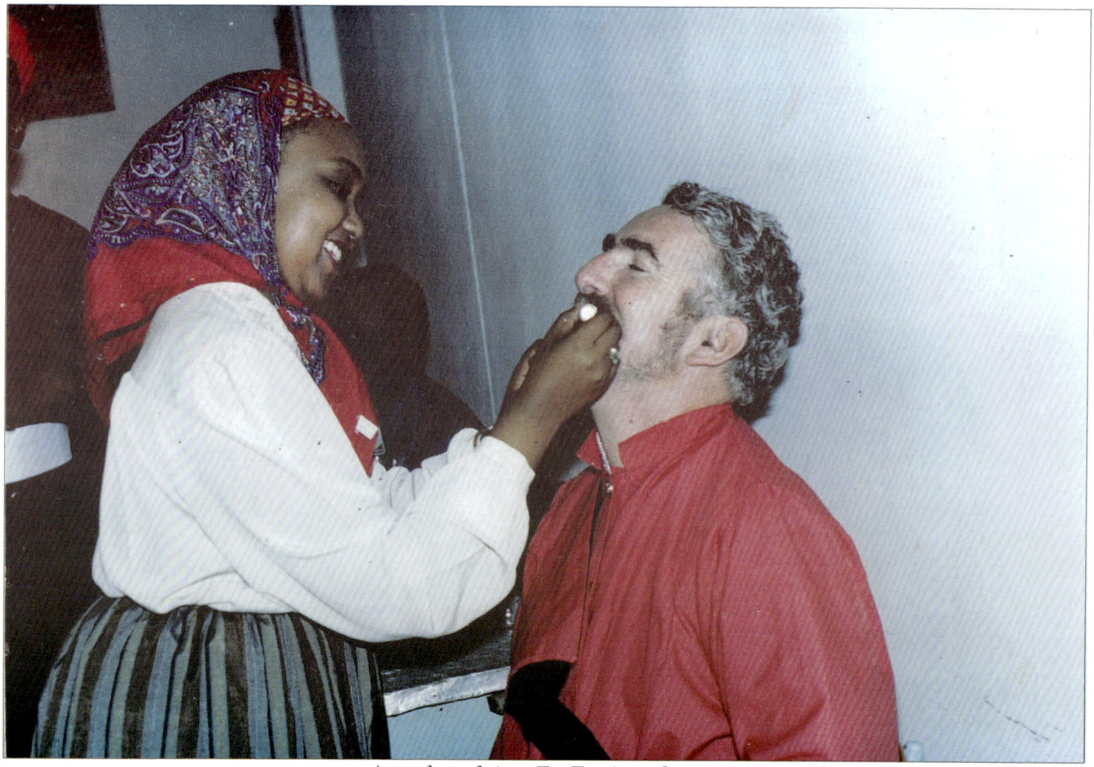

A student doing Fr. Tom's make-up

Scout Investiture at St. Mary's.
In attendance are Mr. Ossie Fernandes, Fr. Tom Hogan and headmaster, Fr. Eddie O'Farrell

Cub Scouts give Fr. Tom a bouquet and a garland of flowers on his final day as Headmaster

Some ground staff members welcome my niece, Sergeant Ruth Cassin, on her visit enroute to Namibia with the Irish Government jet

Mr. Obaga, Mr. Boli, Mrs. Dias and students at Fr. Tom's last Junior Assembly

Fr. Tom Hogan, Ossie Fernandes and Myrill Conitz in the Loita Hills scouting for new destinations for school safaris

Prize Day 1995. Incoming Headmaster, Fr. Michael McMahon, District Leader, Fr. Larry Shine, and outgoing Headmaster, Fr. Tom Hogan

Mrs. Cissy Toscano receives a long service award from Fr. Tom

Fr. Tom is congratulated by District Leader, Fr. Larry Shine, on his 13 years service in St. Mary's School

very few European pupils at that time, so it did not take us long to find out his name. I called the student who was from Hungary to my office and told him: *"Now, we know how the gag was done. Please call all the others involved. We have their names."*
Of course, we did not have any names except his. However, I was lucky and all the culprits turned up at my office. I greeted each one, as if I was expecting them. I talked about the gag, saying that it was the best one in years. However, because of the civil unrest in the city, they had frightened many pupils, staff and domestic workers. Had I dived to the ground, we could have had a serious situation on our hands. I told them that their parents would all be called to discuss the matter.

The culprits told us how they had done the gag. They timed how long it took for the headmaster to walk from his office, climb up the steps to the podium and greet the assembly. They had made a delayed action fuse and had practiced until they knew just how long the fuse needed to be for a 90-second delay. When all was prepared, they waited for April 1st and went up into the water tower until the bell rang for assembly and then lit the fuse. They rushed down to their class assembly line and made sure that they greeted their teacher and stood right beside her.

The parents were called and they agreed that the joke could have had greater implications. The students were suspended for a short time, while acknowledging the great idea of a delayed action fuse; we reminded them of the dangerous outcomes that could have taken place from their actions. Their parents understood our reasons for the suspension and all was forgiven.

Camping adventures; the Surprise Club

I led many adventures on various camping safaris during my thirteen years at St Mary's. The Principal of the primary school, Ossie Fernandez often accompanied me as did his wife, Winnie, who was also a primary teacher in our school. She was particularly good when working with art and on photographic trips. Camping was a great way to get to know the students. I saw some students trying to find a light switch in their tents! It gave students an opportunity to see their own country and its fabulous wildlife.

We shared our knowledge and over the years we became quite knowledgeable about all forms of wildlife. Winnie and Ossie helped to develop my knowledge of birds and Ossie showed us how to recognise and track the spoor of animals. As time went on, we purchased books on trees, birds and animals, wild flowers and insects.

Early on in my time in St Mary's, when Cormac O'Brolchain was headmaster, he asked us to organise various clubs for the students. All types of clubs were started, such as bridge, chess, mechanics and cookery.

Brother Gerard from Uganda said he would like to start an Ornithology Club. Gerard had done his biological studies in Aberdeen University and was very knowledgeable and an experienced and likeable teacher. I told him it was a great idea, but we should call the club 'The Surprise Club', otherwise I feared that the club might get very few members. We told the students that all who joined were guaranteed to get a surprise! So sure enough, I got 20 victims to join the club and Brother Gerard started to explain to them what the club was about. The club members were very surprised to learn that they were to study all about birds. Within a short time, he had photocopied line drawings of the ten most common birds in Kenya. He encouraged the students to colour in the feathers. As they went along, they got to know the names of the individual feathers, the different types of beaks and feet of the birds.

The highlight of the club was a trip to Lake Nakuru, which is famous for its bird life. I was the driver of the mini-bus and I noticed, in just one term, that they had acquired both an interest and knowledge of ornithology that was remarkable. I resolved to become as good as, if not better than them. I followed Brother Gerard's method and eventually became quite good at ornithology and it has remained an abiding interest.

One day, I received a letter from a parent. She told me that her younger son had recently been on one of our camping trips. She had not taken much notice on her son's return, but when he continued to recount our many adventures, she decided to put pen to paper. I remember some lines of the letter: "*…boys become men on such trips and girls become women*" The last line of her letter was: "*Thank you for taking John on the trip, and would you please note that I have an older son in Form Three.*"

Hippos run quickly!

Once, I was in Tsavo National Park, which is one of the largest Wildlife parks in the world. We arranged for a trip for altar servers and took the opportunity to deepen their faith. If you climb up to Roaring Rocks, you will have an extraordinary view out over the valley and across to the Yatta Plateau. It is God's own country, completely untouched, just as He left it. It was there that we took the opportunity to celebrate a Mass at dawn.

We had been out game-spotting since dawn, but we had had little luck. However, I knew of an area near the Tsavo River where we would surely see hippos. I parked the school van as near as I could to the river and then led the seventeen pupils towards the riverbank. Now visitors are not allowed to leave their vehicles in most National Parks, except in a few designated areas such as camp sites or a viewing point. We saw lots of hippo, sure enough, but something made me look behind me and to my horror I saw a large hippo coming out of the bush towards the river. I knew that this was a very dangerous situation because Hippos can get very angry when they find you blocking their way to the river. We quickly ran towards the car. The boys were faster than I was, but I ducked behind a tree and stood perfectly still. I was wearing green bush clothes and hoped that the hippo with his poor eyesight might not have spotted me. I waited until he was near the tree and then darted as fast as I could to the car. On the way, I met one of the teachers, sauntering along the road. "Run quickly, Sister Nancy, there's a hippo coming," …and run we did and made the safety of the car.

That evening, they started a dance around the camp fire and did a great imitation of the hippos which we had seen earlier during the day through the glass wall of the underwater viewing tank in Mzima Springs. However, after the dance I told them *"Gentlemen, it is called censorship. You can't tell your parents exactly what happened today. You just saw lots of hippos. If your parents find out what really happened, this may well be our last trip."* They kept their word and that was the last I heard of it.

Turkana odyssey, a hospital in the middle of the desert and a surprise birthday party

I was fortunate to get some funding from a German charity who wanted Kenyan children to be given the opportunity to discover and learn about the wildlife in their own country. We made a plan to visit Lake Turkana, which is the largest permanent desert lake and also the largest alkaline lake in the world.

Interested students would be chosen for their skills. We would not bring any passengers. It would be vital that the group was able to function as a team and able to get along well, as we would be together in a truck or camp for long periods. Lake Turkana has many scorpions and vipers. We would have to be alert when in camp. The students would have to do some fundraising to pay their share of the trip. Some set up a car washing facility outside their church. We had little trouble in getting a group interested. I was very pleased to have Kevin and Stuart Behrens, two of my nephews from South Africa, joining the trip. It was wonderful to be able to share this remarkable journey with them and it cemented our friendship.

However, first we needed a suitable vehicle – we would have to cross the Chalbi desert in order to reach the pass at North Horr. I went to see Dick Hedges, the manager of the Turkana Bus Company. He had a fleet of ancient 4x4 Mercedes ex- troop carriers, which had been converted for overland journeys from Europe to Africa. This particular bus that we chartered had made the journey from London to Cape Town on a number of occasions and it bore all the scars of the journeys. The truck normally carried sixteen tourists. However, I convinced Dick to let me fill his truck with twenty two pupils and two teachers. He agreed and the deal was done. I was wise enough to choose a few smaller students, so that we could squeeze them into some of the tight corners of the bus.

In view of the difficult terrain and the remoteness of our destination, I arranged that all of us would become members of The Flying Doctor service. We would have a walkie talkie, known as an "over-over", on board with which we could make a radio call to the Flying Doctor if required. As I registered the group, I noticed that one student would be turning sixteen during the trip and therefore would be missing out on his birthday. I said nothing but put a bar of chocolate into the cold box of the truck and kept it for future reference.

I made contact with the manager of Kenya Breweries. Fortunately, his two sons had previously travelled with us to Tsavo Wildlife Park. I requested some sponsorship and was given two full crates of beer to slake the teachers 'thirst'. I promised him that each student would have a soft drink every evening of the trip. It was difficult to keep that promise, but I just about managed it.

Bright and early one morning, the huge Turkana Bus trundled up the road to the school compound. It was so high, with all the camping gear tied up on the roof carrier, that it nearly brought down the telephone line as it went in through the school gates. One of the crew quickly climbed up on top of the truck and with the help of a sweeping brush, just made enough space for the vehicle to slip under the line. My team of students was ready to board. It took us some time to learn how to pack all our gear and as the days went by, we improved and there was more room for us in the truck.

Each evening, we stopped before nightfall and made camp. Some students went collecting firewood, remembering to be careful to look out for scorpions and snakes. Some other students helped the cook to prepare the meals. We continued on our journey, crossed the Mathews Range and went over the North Horr Pass. Here, we found a camp site all ready prepared and a staff member, who looked after the camp and had freshly baked bread for us in his charcoal oven. The smell of freshly baked bread wafted across the camp. We were invited to tuck in and were given hot lemon tea to quench our thirst. It reminded me of the story I heard about my Uncle 'Doggie' O'Gorman-Russell who served in the British 8th Army in the Sahara desert during the Second World War. He used to say that in the desert, they quenched their thirst with red hot tea.

We continued on our journey and crossed over the last pass to reach Lake Turkana and had a vision – a lake of aquamarine blue surrounded by hills – a most extra-ordinary sight; I will never forget that electric blue colour of the lake. This is why Lake Turkana is sometimes referred to as the Jade Sea.

Soon we were by the lake and jumped into the water, while some kept a wary look out, watching for crocodiles. A year or two later, our driver was taken by crocs on another trip in the same bathing spot. Swimming in that part of the lake was then forbidden by the authorities.

We set up home in the camp site and we were soon visited by some local children. They came to the perimeter fence and had a look at the tourists – only to find that most of the 'tourists' were African school children like themselves. Soon we heard that a soccer match has been arranged for the following day by one of our students, Aringo Oloo. Very few knew that he was the son of the Minister of Education of Kenya. We all had good fun playing the football match. However, during the match, the wind came up and when the goalie kicked out the ball, it was taken by the wind and went straight back towards the goal.

All too soon, it was time to start our return journey to Nairobi. It takes thirteen hours driving time to cross the Chalbi desert. The driver mechanic asked me to have the group ready for a 5 a.m. departure. At 4 a.m., I set up my small but powerful music machine known as a 'ghetto blaster' and played the cowboy song 'Back in the saddle again' in order to wake up the students. After three rounds of the song, all were awake! We struck camp while our cook made us breakfast and then we were off. Only two five minutes stops were made on the journey across the Chalbi. We succeeded in crossing the desert and camped in the bush. However, it had been very hot during the day as we drove across the desert and a few of the students were not feeling 100%. I handed out a few pain killers, gave them gallons of hot, sweet lemon tea, some food and we left it at that.

Nevertheless, during the night, the driver mechanic called me to say that Patrick, one of the students, was not well. I went to the tent and called on Patrick to come out. He was unable to, so we simply pulled the mattress and out he came. We had no idea what was wrong with him. Patrick already had his appendix removed the previous year, yet he was complaining of serious pain in his side. I wondered what to do, we considered calling the Flying Doctor but normally they will not fly unless they have spoken with a nurse or doctor. I asked the driver where the nearest medical facility was. He said 'Once a month, there is a nurse in a clinic, about two hours down the road and I think the day is tomorrow'.

I decided we would try it and again the students had an early call. We put mattresses on the floor of the truck and laid out our patient. Imagine my amazement when just two hours later, in the dusty town of Wajir, we found a complete modern hospital. I went in search of help and soon found an Italian Consolata Sister. I explained to her who I was, dirty as I was and dressed in dark green bush clothes – she did not seem to be worried. She said *'Father, you are welcome but there is no doctor on duty today, however, I am a nurse.'* She told us to bring our patient inside. She had a quick look at him and announced *'There is no doctor on duty today, but in five minutes a doctor will be here'*. A few minutes later, a young Italian volunteer doctor arrived, dressed in freshly laundered clothes as if he had just been called from his bed. He examined Patrick and gave him some medicine. I was told how to look after him and we were told that we could travel with him to Nairobi. I thanked the doctor for coming on duty, when he had only just returned from a three day stay in the Chalbi desert. I went to make some payments. But the Sister refused, saying that they were glad to help. I told her, *"This boy's parents run a paint factory in Nairobi and when they hear how you have helped him, I hope they are going to give you enough paint sufficient for three of the wards"*.

We made a bed for Patrick in the truck so that he could rest. He slept most of that day and each time he awoke, we gave him water. He recovered somewhat and after two days, we arrived back safe and sound in St Mary's School. All the parents were there, except for the parents of Patrick. I was just too tired to start driving him home; after all we had just travelled two thousand five hundred kilometres. Viloo Nowregee, one of our teachers, kindly offered to bring the student home.

A few days passed and I was still expecting a phone call, maybe to say thanks, maybe to ask how I had managed to get medical help in the middle of a desert! However, no call was made and those good people were never thanked. I didn't need to be thanked but I often wished that some gesture was made to those good Sisters who had a wonderful hospital, functioning in a most remote and torturous terrain and climate.

Subsequently, I have used this story, disguised of course, to illustrate a point when talking about the story of the ten lepers and only one came back to give thanks. There is one other event that I use when commenting on the story of the ten lepers. In my first year of teaching in Blackrock College, Dublin, I was asked to accompany the scouts on their annual camp. I had never been a scout but had always wanted to be one. However, bouts of asthma and hay fever as a young boy made my mother reluctant to give me permission to join the scouts.

So, off I went with the scouts to Lake Windermere in the Lake District of England. It was a fabulous setting and our camp overlooked the lake. One day, we had a swimming festival and I was the lifeguard. There were students in the water when, suddenly, the Scoutmaster said *"Quick, someone is going down"*. I threw off my jumper and glasses and dashed into the lake. I was able to successfully rescue the student and on return to shore, I saw that my watch was still on my wrist. Oops! It looked as if it was full of water!

On my return to Ireland, I went into

O'Connell Street and gave my watch to O'Connor's Jeweller's for repair and was told that it would cost ten shillings to repair. When I went to collect it after one week, I was surprised to see the student, whom I had saved, standing behind the counter. The student told his dad *"this is Mr Hogan who saved me when I was drowning in Lake Windemere'*. "Oh thank you very much", he said *"I will only charge you half price for repairing the watch"*. Someone told me afterwards that I should have replied, *"Next time, I will make sure not to rush out into the water before checking if I have taken off my watch!"*

Back to the story of our Turkana trip: We camped in Samburu game reserve on the last night of our trip and I remembered our birthday boy. I went to the truck and found the bar of chocolate that I had put in the bottom of the cold box at the beginning of our journey. I got a knife, a plate and a bush lamp and arrived at the camp fire. Our birthday boy was very surprised when we presented his 'cake' and asked him to blow out the bush lamp and told him to cut the bar of chocolate into twenty four equal pieces as we sang 'Happy Birthday'. He told me afterwards, that he had realised that he would be missing his birthday party by going on the Turkana trip but he really wanted this adventure. He said that this surprise party was the best birthday party that he had ever had.

We broke a leaf spring on the back suspension as we continued on the rough roads. The lorry was now leaning to one side and I wondered how we would get out of this situation. Not to worry, 'Captain' Walter, our mechanic driver, made an ingenious repair by wrapping the set of springs together with a long strip of tyre tube. The repair enabled us to travel the last seven hundred kilometres of our safari. Father John Mahon, from Kildare, our school chaplain who was with us, produced a mouth organ and a sheet of Christmas Carols which we sang on the last hour of our long journey. It is a memory that I carry still.

However, we ended up arriving very late in Nairobi and just before we arrived at school, Michael Moloney, the Principal of Secondary School, announced that there was to be a new headmaster in St Mary's and he told the students. That is how I became headmaster of the school while on the Turkana Bus. There was meant to be an official handover and a meal. I made the last fifteen minutes of the meal and was able to drive my predecessor, Fr Eddie O'Farrell, to Nairobi Airport for his return flight to Ireland. It had been a long day.

Lake Nakuru

A trip for bird watchers or Bird Fanciers, as the club was known in school, was planned for Lake Naivasha. I invited my friend Fr Camillus Kane, who originally hailed from Trim, Co. Meath to join me there. However, when I got to Lake

Naivasha, I found the campsite full of tourists, so we headed further up the Rift valley to Lake Nakuru, which is also famous for bird watching. Hundreds of thousands of flamingos flock there regularly and can be seen feeding in the shallows at the edge of the lake. From the viewing point on a nearby cliff, the many flamingos look like a pink necklace around the edge of the lake.

At that time, Camillus was living quite near Nakuru and was surprised to find himself camping, while we could see the lights of his home at Wanyanyoro Mission up on the hills to the west. Wanyanyoro means 'the Place of the Chains' In the days of slavery, the chains would be removed at this village as the slavers knew that the people would not run. If they wanted to live, they had to stay with their masters. Camillus wondered what he was doing on a cold night, sitting around a camp fire, with warm feet but a cold back because of the biting wind. He could have been up in his lovely warm mission house!

Camillus was a great one to tell ghost stories. He went on about the "banshee". With suitable shrieks, he illustrated his story. Camillus was voted the one with the best ghost stories. Just to get the atmosphere going, Ossie Fernandez and I used to frequently look over our shoulders. Students would ask *'What's wrong? Oh nothing, just thought I heard something in the bush'* we replied. All this helped getting everyone in the mood for ghost stories.

Eventually, the story telling was over and it was time to get into our tents. About an hour or so afterwards, I was woken up by one of the students to tell me that young Hital Patel was having nightmares. He just could not get himself back into his tent and spent most of the night huddled up near the fire. Ossie and I had to stay with him and we sipped a little whiskey, just to keep away the cold. Hital told me "You are going to be the next headmaster of St Mary's". I told him not to be ridiculous. However, some years later, when I found myself as head of the school, Hital, by then a senior student, came to me and reminded me that he had predicted this many years previously. How true!

Before Hital had completed his secondary school, Camillus, died in an unfortunate accident when his car exploded in flames – he was only thirty six years of age. It was a strange turn of events and a difficult time for us at school. The loss of Father Camillus was devastating for us Spiritans and I often remember him and those wonderful days we had together.

Amboseli Game Reserve: kites, frights and cello players

Just outside Amboseli Game Park, there is a very fine tented camp, owned by a professional photographer. During the off season, the camp owner allowed a few selected schools to use his camp – it was very well set up and ideal for our purposes.

We have used the camp on a number of occasions. Once, I was there with a group of student photographers from school. Early morning would find us in the park, as the best photos were taken soon after dawn. Later on in the morning, the light would be very flat and the photos would not be the best. Now, you can't spend all day in a mini bus with seventeen students, so after our two hour trip in the morning, we would come back to camp for breakfast. What an amount of food those young people could put away. I used to tell them that they had hollow legs!

We had to invent ways of keeping the pupils occupied during the day before we set off for the evening run into the park. We engaged them in various activities and sometimes Ossie Fernandes taught the younger students how to make kites which they flew on a nearby dirt airstrip. At other times, we taught them how to make small toy boats using twigs, leaves, shells, in fact, any natural product that they could find around the camp. The boys had fun racing the boats down the river.

After a long day, the students eventually went to bed after camp fire songs and ghost stories were over. I had been sipping a little whiskey from a hip flask which used to belong to Major Meagher. During the Second World War, many of our priests served in the Allied forces as chaplains and Fr Meagher had been one of those chaplains. I left my gear on the camp table and retired to my tent. The next morning, we found that an animal had been in the camp and had knocked over the hip flask and the remaining whiskey had spilled on my map of the area. What a loss!

I forgot about the incident until the following Friday, when we had Junior School Assembly. There were six hundred primary pupils in the hall, all sitting in rows, class by class. It was Ossie's turn to take the assembly and he had asked me to do a song or two with my guitar. I was still up on the stage when he asked one of the campers from the Amboseli trip to tell of the adventures. So the student started and told them all about the safari *"and when we got up in the morning, we found that a civet cat had knocked over Fr Hogan's bottle of whiskey"*. The teachers told me that my face was becoming redder and redder as the story went on – I was wondering what was coming next! I was just thinking of the younger ones telling their mums and dads *"and Fr Hogan had this huge bottle of whiskey and it was knocked over by a lion and it …."*

At that camp, Ossie used to teach younger pupils how to make kites using pieces of bamboo and rice paper. Later on, I was surprised to find out that secondary pupils were also quite happy to make and fly kites. It was a Saturday and the kite making was going on and Ossie was in charge. I had some time off and was sitting at my little table outside my tent, writing some letters to my family. It was all very peaceful and I was very relaxed. Suddenly, Andrew, one of the pupils rushed up the path holding a large tea towel over his hand! I had a quick look and saw quite a deep cut.

We were over one hundred kilometres from the nearest health centre and it was Saturday afternoon. Would there be anyone there if we went? I decided that there was a real possibility of travelling on that rough road for nothing. So I decided to stitch the young man myself. I had a comprehen-sive first aid box that my sister Anne, who is a pharmacist, had helped me fill and I remember she made me buy all sorts of things which I thought would never be used, such as butterfly stitches and petroleum gauze bandages for burns. I remember complaining about her extravagance, but she assured me that one day I would be thankful. That day had arrived and I closed the wound with a couple of butterfly stitches. I wondered how we would keep the wound clean over the weekend. Now it happened to be the time of the break-dancing craze and one of my pupils had a brand new break-dancing glove still in its plastic wrapping. Therefore, I asked Andrew to wear the glove for the rest of the weekend.

On arrival back in St Mary's, I wondered what I would say to Dr Munuya, Andrew's father. What would he think of my stitching! I told him our tale and he said *"Well he is stitched now and it's too late to do anything about it, we'll just have to wait and see how good you are at sewing"* Some years later, I was watching our school orchestra playing. St Mary's is the only school in Kenya with a full orchestra. Andrew was playing the cello and I looked at his hand and there was no scar – I felt proud of my work and reminded myself to thank my sister Anne for her extravagance!

Tsavo National Park – Baboons like crisps!

At that time, transport was a difficulty for some students of St Mary's School, so together with parents, we organised a fundraising and purchased a brand new fifty six seater bus. This would be used daily to collect students from different parts of Nairobi city, to bring them to school in the morning and return them to their homes in various parts of the city in the evening.

I knew just the place to test out the bus – Tsavo National Park – a favourite haunt of mine, since I had lived beside it for seven years and knew the area very well. I had found out that any school who were members of The Wildlife Clubs of Kenya had free entry to any of the Kenyan National Parks. All we had to do was pay a small fee for each pupil to camp and teachers went for free. It was my first major camp. I had thirty pupils and three teachers with me.

Unfortunately, I had just undergone some surgery on my knee and my leg was heavily bandaged but I knew that I just had to go.

When we eventually arrived at the Tsavo Park camp site, we pitched the tents in a single line, with teachers camped at either end. I pitched my tent in the centre, so that I could keep an eye on things. We parked our smart new bus parallel to the tents and lit the campfire in the centre of the area.

On the first night after all were fed and bedded down, I was asleep in my tent when I awoke with the sneaking suspicion that something was up! So I stuck my head out of my small pup tent and was alarmed to see a herd of elephants with young, picking their way between the tents. This was a very dangerous situation, as elephants with young will protect them. I had visions of a few of my pupils being squashed by an elephant's foot! Just imagine trying to explain that to an angry parent! I hobbled out and went up the line to the last tent where two teachers were sleeping. I shook the tent and they woke up. I whispered that we had a problem. So we put some more branches on the campfire and then went towards the elephants with some branches and a shovel of live coals and started another fire. As the smoke from the fires wafted down towards the elephants, they lumbered off as quietly as they had come.

The following morning I gave the students a censored version of what had happened during the night. Later on that day, we had some more surprise adventures. On arrival back from a game run, we found a troop of baboons running up and down the tents and swinging from the tent poles. Some of the tents were ripped as the baboons went inside to get some crisps and sweets that the boys had carelessly left around. It was a good lesson to us – don't leave food around the camp; otherwise wild animals will come and look for their share! The students just had to manage with the remaining tents which were still intact and the trip continued without further incident and we returned home safely after a great adventure.

A few days after our return, a kind parent rang me up and told me he had heard from his son of our adventures and of the baboons damaging some of the tents. He asked me to deliver the damaged tents to his workshop, where the tents were expertly repaired... at no cost.

Tsavo Adventure – Shake Down Cruise and Death Soup

Parents were requesting more school transport and we had just taken delivery of another brand new school bus. In those days, you first purchased a chassis and then looked for "body builders" to build a body according to your specifications for the vehicle. Frank Caffrey and I designed the vehicle body ourselves so that it would be suitable for school trips, including camping. Three roll bars were designed to be built into the body section, while lockable storage boxes were fitted under the floor. Together with Fr Frank Caffrey and Ossie Fernandes, Principal of the Primary school, we set off with seventeen secondary pupils. We purposely chose experienced campers to join us in the trip which was meant to be the shake-down cruise for the new bus – little did I know what a shake-down it was to be!

We entered the Park at Maktau Gate and as I was registering our group in the 'Entry Book' to the Park, we noticed that no other vehicles had entered during the previous three days. "Great, we have that section of the park all to ourselves."

We pitched our tents in two neat rows facing Lake Chale. Right behind the lake stood the Pare Mountains in Tanzania. The trip was going well, but we noticed that during our day trip in and around Lake Chale, that the clutch was slipping a bit. I managed to adjust the clutch and it was working a little better. We arrived back from one excursion to find that our camp had been destroyed – all of our tents were knocked flat. A sudden tropical storm had erupted and in three minutes had wreaked havoc on our lovely camp. Some damage was caused, but we managed to rebuild our camp.

On our return, at about half way point between our campsite and Maktau gate, the clutch gave up completely. What were we to do? Unfortunately our water supplies were low, with just enough for the last day of the trip. I realised that no one would just drive by, so I would have to walk out to the Park gate to get help. No one was going to help us except ourselves! A discussion took place among us teachers as to the wisdom of this action. We were in a National Park with lots of wild animals. Nevertheless, if one has a home to return to, it can strengthen you to make the most difficult journey. So, together with two of the bravest students, Satnam Singh and Peter Kyalo, I trekked to the gate. As we left the party and the broken down bus, we were given a litre of water between the three of us. We armed ourselves as best we could; Satnam had a Masai sword, Peter had a dagger and a sling shot and I had a sharp 'panga' (large slashing knife) which I thought might come in handy.

We met many wild animals on our twenty kilometre walk, including buffalo, and eventually, completely exhausted, we made it to the safety of Maktau gate where some of the wardens and staff lived. A Park Ranger stood outside the Park Office watching us coming from a distance, as we made our weary way up the airstrip. All we wanted was water, which we were given but advised to take our time drinking. With true African hospitality, he requested his wife to prepare some food for us and gave each one a sack on which to lie down and rest after our epic walk. Because we were so exhausted, the sacks became the softest mattresses that we had ever had.

There was no vehicle available to tow our school bus to safety, but by evening the Anti Poaching Unit returned from a day patrol. I managed to convince the Officer in Charge to go back into the Park and tow the bus out. He told the patrol *"You can have a five minutes break and then we are going to rescue those students"*.

We started off and with the one headlamp blazing, were able to see the road. In the distance, we saw a small light and as we neared the school bus, we could see a blazing fire that had been started to keep wild animals away. Never were students so pleased to see their teacher! We towed the bus back to Maktau and as we drove past the airstrip, we saw some lions stretch out, relaxing. We arrived safely and were told that we could pitch our tents beside the airstrip. The students were still thinking of the lions we had seen at the other end of the airstrip and announced that they would sleep in the bus. However, the teachers and I pitched our tents and prepared for a well earned rest.

The warden arrived at our makeshift camp to see how we were getting along. He brought with him forty litres of water and told us that was all the water he could spare and that it would have to do us until a rescue vehicle arrived to bring us back home to the school. The students and teachers were starving by this time. It was meant to be the end of the trip and we should have been at our homes but I had a look in the cook box to see what ingredients I could find that might help me. I had two carrots and a few onions, one packet of soup and a few stock cubes. I started preparing soup; I had to make sufficient volume but had to be careful not to use too much of our precious water supply. I remembered that I had some tins of French beans and also a can of peas. In they went, together with some of the precious liquid. I threw in our last remaining packets of long life milk. Then I remembered that I had half a bottle of altar wine, which would help. The soup was eventually ready. The students said it was 'death soup', which in students' language meant it was excellent!

I forgot about the lions and had a good sleep. We eventually managed to contact the school on the following day and the headmaster at the time Fr Eddie O'Farrell was much relived to hear from us. He had waited up the whole night, wondering where we were. He was very happy to hear that we were on our way back. We had to leave the bus in the Park and returned to Nairobi by another way, like the 'Three Wise Men'. I wondered though what I would say to parents on our arrival. However, I needn't have worried as they were very happy to see us return safe and sound and welcomed their sons home.

During the following school week, I rang all the parents to explain what had happened and to apologise. I needn't have worried. They had all heard of our adventures and were happy that their children had had such a fantastic and exciting trip!

Rumuruti camp: Another use for a filing cabinet

One of our students, Charles Cardovilles, was a keen camper and suggested that we go and camp on his family ranch up at Rumuruti. Charles's great grandfather was a Greek who has entered Kenya as a trader and he made his way down Africa, through Ethiopia, on foot.

There were game animals, including elephant, in the Rumaruti ranch so we would have to be careful. I looked for some students who were interested in this trip, reminding them that it was not for the faint-hearted! There would be a lot of walking, as there were few roads on the ranch.

We arrived at the campsite, which Charles had identified. We were very impressed by the dry toilet which he had set up for us – it was a hole in the ground, covered by the drawer of a filing cabinet with a good stout toilet seat on top! It was the first time that I had seen a filing cabinet used in such a manner. In fact, it was one of the best uses I have seen for a filing cabinet! The toilet area was encircled by a wall of bush. You had to sing or whistle while using the toilet, otherwise you might get visitors during your performance!

As it turned out, we were not able to do all the walking that we had planned as some of the elephants were in 'musth' – having high levels of testosterone. This term meant that it was mating time and they would be both dangerous and aggressive. We enjoyed the camp thoroughly and the older students taught a lot of camping skills to the younger members of the party.

A few dirty words

Pokot is a remote area and the few confrères that we had there seldom had visitors. I used to visit Fr. John Kevin and Fr. Sean McGovern regularly. Once, John asked me to celebrate Mass on Sunday and since I didn't speak Ki-Pokot, the Pokot language, I said I would celebrate the Mass in slow and easy Kiswahili. I was going well enough and the people were beginning to respond. When I got to the sermon, I began to speak slowly and very deliberately. Just after reading the gospel I meant to say 'Now I will say a few words on the Gospel' but I was amazed to hear myself saying 'Now I will say a few dirty words'. The people were very good and no one laughed. They knew exactly what I was trying to say!

Bike trek Safari

One morning, during my term as headmaster, Nigel Arransen of Abercrombie and Kent – the internationally recognised 'Safari Outfitters' arrived at my office. He announced *"You are the only headmaster in Kenya who can get himself and ten students together with bicycles and be ready to travel with me this coming week-end!"*

Nigel had been educated at St Mary's

and he went on to explain that he was looking for a group of students and their headmaster to help him test a 'Bike Trek Safari' that Abercrombie were considering doing for visitors.

I had already led 'Bike Treks' with my nieces and nephews in Ireland over a number of years. I thought this was an interesting proposition indeed. There was a very small fee involved to cover the cost of food and I had little trouble in getting ten willing students. At lunchtime that Friday, a huge fully stocked lorry and a Land Rover arrived in the school. We loaded the bicycles and gear into the specially adapted trailer of the Land Rover and off we set for Kajiado country. Envious students watched us pack our gear and wished us well on our trip. They reluctantly went back to class, while we went off to a new outdoor classroom for the week-end!

As soon as we left the main Nairobi-Mombasa road, we started to cycle, while the lorry went ahead to set up camp in Masai country. The Land Rover stayed behind us cyclists and picked up any stragglers who got left behind because of tiredness or punctures.

On arrival, we were very pleased to see a really organised camp – the grass had been cut to drive away snakes and other unwelcome guests. The mess tent even had cloths on the tables! This was going to be luxury camping and Masai warriors had been arranged to stand guard during the night.

Each day, we cycled on the Masai cattle trails and over the weekend we had twenty eight punctures between us – which we thought could have been a record. The bike technician who was with us had a busy time in camp, repairing all the bicycles.

It was around Easter time and I knew that a friend of mine and the son of one of our teachers, Dr Sudir Vinayak was practicing for the Kenya safari car rally in the area. Unknown to the students, I told Vinayak, the navigator, where we would be cycling. In the distance, we began to hear the sound of a vehicle. I urged caution and we went to the side of the track. Suddenly, amid a huge cloud of dust, the rally car roared up to us and skidded to a stop. It was very exciting for the students to meet the Japanese ace who was the driver. We were surprised at the high temperature of the car and we saw the driver and co-driver drenched with sweat. They opened the bonnet and showed us the red hot turbo, glowing with heat.

Nigel had someone making a promotional video and he was making a record of the trip. We were watching the video some days after and were pleased to see a shot of us cycling on a long stretch of track. We were more than surprised to see a herd of buffalo that crossed the road when we had just passed. We hadn't heard a sound or seen sight of them until we saw it on the screen. This trip was the start of many a bike trek and cycling is a great way to see Africa.

A story of bravery

Gerald Muriuki was a pupil in the primary class of St Mary's and I was at first, his teacher, then his principal and a few years later I became his headmaster. When he was in primary school, Gerald used to fall down for no known reason. We informed the parents about this and they had him checked and eventually he was sent to St Thomas's Hospital in London. It turned out that Gerald had an inoperable tumour on the brain. On his return, he was in Nairobi Hospital and I could often be found at the foot of his bed at evening time, writing letters and reading documents. Now and then, Gerald would wake up from his coma and find me there and talk. I was there quite a number of times and we gave him the Sacrament of the Sick. As time got more difficult, it was clear that he was going to die. He was unconscious when I confirmed him. I remember asking his sister Carol what confirmation name he should be given and she said *"Let his name be Jude"* – the patron saint of hopeless cases.

One time, I was sitting beside the end of the bed when Gerald woke up and we began talking. He asked me *"Please tell me; am I going to die?"* He looked me straight in the eye and I knew I could tell no lie. I said *"Your time of suffering is coming to an end. Soon, Jesus will come for you and you will be with him. All the pain is going to be over"*. This was the question that he was not prepared to ask his parents.

Some time later, his mother and I were present and he asked his mother to remove the airway tube so that he could speak. He had great difficulty speaking and his voice was just a whisper. I had to lean close to hear him and then he said *"You have helped me so much"*. It upset me to hear that – what had I done? Some time later after he had died I asked his mother *"This boy nearly broke my heart, what had I done? Why had he said that? I had done nothing!"* She replied *"He said that because you were there when he woke up out of his coma, he found his teacher, his principal and now his headmaster"*. This taught me that sometimes all you have to do is to be there.

A difficult case in discipline

An event happened in St Mary's school that reminds me that sometimes it is the students who give you the most trouble who are the very ones who give you the greatest satisfaction when you see them doing well in later life.

It was St Patrick's Day and one of our students, originally from Ireland, asked if he could attend his father's book launch. His father had just written a book to be published in Nairobi on of all things, St Patrick! In order to encourage me to give him permission, he reminded me that I would be attending the St Patrick's Ball with his parents that very evening, which was being organised by the Irish Society.

It was a Friday afternoon. While I was teaching class, my secretary came to the door and said *"I think you best come down to your office"*. Down I went to find the manager of a nearby health club in my office. He said *"It's very simple, there are students from your school in school uniform, boys and girls, smoking, drinking alcohol and they will not leave the club'*. I replied *'I will go down straight away"*.

I quickly located Margaret Ngwalla, the teacher with responsibility for girls, and Mr Onyango, the Dean of the International Baccalaureate class. We drove down and entered the club. I remember walking across the open area in front of the swimming pool at Ratna Health Club. I could feel the close scrutiny of people around the pool as we passed by in our formal clothes. Out of the corner of my eye, I could see the students on the far side of the pool, seated around a table. Glasses of wine were being pushed left and right and packets of cigarettes going over the side of the table. I went straight up to them and said *"Good afternoon, would you please come and see me in my office in the next five minutes?"* There were about seven of them. Now this was a serious situation, they had been taking alcohol, smoking cigarettes and dressed in their school uniform, when they were meant to be at class in school. Of course, among them, I saw my friend from Ireland, who was meant to have been at the launch of his father's book! However, he had decided to organise lunch for some of his friends instead.

On returning to school, Aidan Williams, a teacher friend said to me *"Please do not over-react to this situation"*. I said *"Don't worry; we will do exactly what we normally do. We will establish a Discipline Committee and the students can explain themselves. The committee will investigate and make various recommendations to me as Headmaster and I will decide what to do."*

The committee met and gave me recommendations. I decided that the students would be out of school for one month, would not be allowed to use the library services at school, would not attend the school musical *'Joseph and the Amazing Technicolor Dreamcoat'* which I was producing. They would also not attend the schoolboy rugby final of Kenya.

I began to meet the parents. One student was Ugandan and her ward, the person responsible for her, came from the High Commission and said to me *"This is very embarrassing, this girl is the daughter of a Minister in the Ugandan government. This could be an international incident"*. I felt he was hinting that she should be treated differently. *"Oh yes,* I said, *' just imagine how that is going to look in the Nation Newspaper tomorrow morning. Daughter of a Ugandan Minister caught smoking and drinking during school hours'*. I said *"She is going to get the same punishment as the rest of the students"*. Maybe he thought that I might make an exception for the daughter of a Government Minister. However, one for all and all for one!

One of the girls was the leader of the school orchestra and one of the boys was the percussionist. Some staff and students thought that I might make an exception, since I was the producer of the musical. I knew we would have to manage without them. It was not possible to make exceptions on this occasion.

After it was all over and the students returned, they told me that the thing that hurt the most was not being able to attend the school musical. The other thing they missed was the school rugby final and not being able to see St Mary's winning the School's Cup that year.

A few years later, I had the pleasure of meeting the Irish boy's mother, whose son had organised the lunch at Ratna Fitness Centre. She imparted the good news that her son had just completed his degree in university. Despite the problems he had brought us when in school, he had still managed to get himself through university and graduate. Sometimes, it is the pupils that you try hardest with who are the very ones that give you the most satisfaction. It is great to see students doing well, despite difficulties in studies or discipline in school.

Refugees –
my new brother and sister

In 1995, during my last year as headmaster, huge numbers of refugees began to arrive in Kenya from eleven different countries. Some of the countries were Rwanda, Somalia, Sudan, Uganda and Bosnia. Bosnia was the one that surprised me most.

I was inundated with parents trying to place children in schools. Many of them did not have any money to pay school fees. Paddy Leonard, the Kenya representative of World Mercy Fund, came to my rescue and gave half of the school fees while the school matched the donation with a half scholarship. I was able to give places to thirty five students from six years of age to eighteen years. None of these children spoke English and this meant that thirty five classes had a student who would not understand what the teacher was saying. I was not the most popular headmaster with some teachers! I was surprised to find myself being criticised by some. I wondered if they really knew what we were trying to do in St Mary's. I had to go begging in other schools for places for young girl students, as we only took girls for the last two years of secondary education. The nearby Loreto Convent School was very helpful and we managed to place all the students.

In an effort to help the new students, we gave each primary student two older pupils who would be their big brother and sister. After classes had finished, the students would look for their 'younger brother' and bring him back to his classroom to try and read the homework on the blackboard. They would then help the younger one do his homework. It worked well and the younger ones quickly made friends with their new 'brother and sister'.

Some of these students spoke of their experiences and indeed some of them unintentionally revealed the trauma they had suffered when they drew pictures in art class. We quickly recognised drawing of rifles with a banana shaped magazine as 'AK 47' rifles! A few of them wrote of their experiences and Chantal has given me permission to publish her story.

Dear Father Tom Hogan,

You have been, you are and you always will be the one who brought back hope into our lives. We came here to Nairobi as a desperate refugee family that had nothing more to live for, whose future was looking cloudy and grey.

Personally, I had no hope. I had lost almost everything I cared for, my friends, my house, my country, my childhood, my dogs and especially I had no hope to ever go back to school (to a good school at least). My life had actually come to a standstill.

Then, you came into our lives. Rather, the Almighty directed our father's footsteps to your door and you didn't hesitate to welcome him and help us. You were the sun that moved away the cloud and made the future look bright again. You brought back the smile and hope into our eyes, interest towards life and the feeling that our future was not that bad after all.

There are no words and no way I know that could possibly express our gratitude. I have been able to continue my studies and to use my talents to the best of my ability.

The only thing I strive for now in my life, is to always be for you a source of pride so that you can never regret having helped me.

Once again thank you.

Chantal Nyandwi

When the time came for me to leave St Mary's, all the refugees came to my office one day to say thanks. They told me that I had welcomed them with a smile when they had first come. They also reminded me, that soon after joining St Mary's, I had gathered all of them to my office one day. They said that I had told them on arrival "You are all very welcome to St Mary's. You have three months to learn English or else you are out!" I have no recollection of the incident but they were sure that it had happened. They presented me with a silk tie, which I still use – it certainly is my favourite.

On the morning of my departure, I was inside the airport in the departure lounge all ready to board the plane. I was most surprised when suddenly I found myself mobbed by the refugee pupils. They were very pleased with themselves and really had one up on me. I asked how they had managed to get into the airport security area as I knew that many of them had no passports! Then Chantal, who was a student leader, told that she had arranged with a senior judge, who just happened to be a parent and got permission for them to enter the departure lounge. They had even brought the youngest pupils along with them. They were very pleased and proud to see me wearing my new silk tie. And so I took the plane for London and left my post of headmaster of a fifteen hundred pupil school and two days later found myself as a student of The Institute of Education in London University and in charge of a coffee club with thirteen members! It was a great change in my life.

Chantal finished school and qualified for university; she settled down in Belgium, has learnt Flemish and became a Belgian citizen. She now works for the European Union.

Our Days at "Saints"

Many years later, I received the following letter from an Ethiopian past student who had gone to great lengths to find me. It does my heart good to read it.

Dear Fr Hogan,
For many years I've wanted to find you. To tell you how much of an impact St Mary's had on me and especially you. As you know, in those days, Ethiopia was not a good place to be and when my dad was transferred back to our country, my mum and I stayed in Nairobi.

Let's say without my dad in the house, I was a disruptive kid at home and didn't concentrate on my studies. If it was not for you and St. Mary's, I know my life would be very different.

I met Martin Wai Waruwai this past weekend in New York City. We reminisced about our days at 'Saints'. You guys were good to us. We are all over the world and we continue to stay in touch, even after not seeing each other for years. I hadn't seen Martin in twenty three years and we picked up right where we left off. That's the bond St Mary's created among its students.

My mom still lives in Nairobi in the same house I grew up in. I'm married and live in Michigan. I got a Bachelor of Science degree in Business Marketing from Indiana University and an MBA from University of Michigan. I've worked for Ford for thirteen years now in my different roles with much success. You should know that many of us are successful because of you and others like you. Thanks for giving us your heart. We hope we make you proud.

I hope we keep in touch. If you have a phone number, it would be great to catch up with you. I hope we meet someday soon.

Tedros Mengiste.

Part 3

BURA-TANA, GARISSA
1996 to 2004

Introduction

In 1995, there was a meeting of Spiritans who were working in Kenya. I was present at that meeting of the extended District Council. We decided to start two new missions in more challenging and needy areas. We believed that more challenging ventures might entice the younger people to get involved, in particular from the East African Province. I was there for that decision and was one of the ones who voted. I was going to vote No because of lack of our personnel. I really wondered where we would get new personnel for these jobs. Then our leader in Kenya, Fr Martin Keane asked for a unanimous vote which would send a message to the rest of the confreres. So I voted to start these new parishes, one was to be in Mukuru shanty town in Nairobi while the other was to be in Tana River District, Coast Province.

Kenya's longest river, the Tana, rises in the forested highlands north of Nairobi and heads north where it is fed by tributaries from Mount Kenya. It then turns east on its one thousand kilometre journey and meanders in a serpentine fashion through the low lying regions of Kenya's Eastern and Coastal Provinces on its way to the Indian Ocean.

Irrigation Settlement Schemes and a new challenge

Over the years, three government irrigation and resettlement schemes have been established along the Tana River, but only the Lake Kenyatta settlement scheme at Mpeketoni still functions. These settlement schemes were started because of the growing problem of landlessness in Central and Western Kenya.

Tenant farmers from twenty eight ethnic groups live in ten villages on the Bura Irrigation and Settlement Project at Bura-Tana, in the Tana River District, Coast Province of Kenya. Near the ten villages, two thousand five hundred indigenous nomadic pastoralists of the Orma tribe live in twenty residential settlements known as 'manyattas'. The scheme was meant to grow cotton, which it did for a number of years. However, by the time we went there in 1995, the scheme had collapsed. In 1986, the World Bank withdrew its involvement from the US $110 million scheme, citing in their report that the Kenyan management capacity was over-centralised and incompetent. No cotton was grown during the ten years I was there. The tenant farmers were left struggling to eke out a miserable existence, helped occasionally with relief food.

Within a short time, we had a new leader for the Spiritans in Kenya, Fr Larry Shine from Ireland. Early one morning, he arrived at St Mary's School and came into the headmaster's office and asked me if I could help him get to Bura-Tana in the Tana River District, which is five hundred kilometres from Nairobi. I said I could and Larry Shine asked me how I would do that. *"I'll hire a plane and a* pilot". "*Well, you had better come as well,*" he added.

A friend enabled me to hire a plane and a pilot. We had to make sure that we landed in the correct airstrip, as the Kenya military had another air strip near Bura-Tana which was off limits. We flew there one Friday morning, just after I had taken the school assembly. I instructed Mrs Darline Masolia, my secretary, to make sure that my office door was kept wide open all day. I left my blazer hanging on the back of the chair, so that the pupils would think that I was around. This was an old trick of Kenya Government civil servants. I always called Masolia by her surname, just in case anybody heard me saying *"Darline, please come into my office!"* It might have been misunderstood!

Our pilot used his Global Positioning System, but after an hour or so, it lost electrical power and suddenly stopped working. I told him that I thought I could fix the loose connection with my trusty Swiss Army knife which had a small screw driver, which I used to fix the connection. We restarted it and made sure that we landed in the correct airstrip. As we flew in, the place looked like Mars! It was an extraordinary sight. No trees could be seen for miles except the ones on the river line of the Tana. The area looked like a desert; there was very little ground cover. In fact, from the air, the land looked brown, as though there was no grass at all.

A few days later, Fr Larry arrived into my office and asked me if I would leave St Mary's and go to Bura-Tana. I had always said that I would return to the bush after St Mary's, so I agreed and Larry invited me to meet the Bishop of the Garissa Diocese. My meeting with Bishop Paul clashed with an invitation that I had received to meet Mother Teresa of Calcutta. Each week a group of our senior students used to do social work in the Eastleigh Home run by Mother Teresa's Order. Fr. John Mahon went instead of me and had a thirty minute meeting with a saint, while I had a half hour meeting with a Bishop! What a contrast!

After the meeting with Larry Shine, I asked him if anyone was going with me to work in the remote area of Bura-Tana. Larry said that Fr Peter Suttle might be available and he promised to go to Uganda where Peter was working at the time and ask him. Peter met him at the airport and during the drive into Kampala, Larry asked the question – *"Will you come back to Kenya and take up a new assignment with Tom Hogan in the Tana River?"* Peter agreed and began to wind up his affairs in Uganda.

I was to go and work in the Tana River district and manage and run five dispensaries. I decided that I would have to prepare myself and I therefore went to London University and did a Master's degree in Education – Health Promotion. So, one October evening in 1995, I found myself among a group of forty students and I was the eldest at forty nine! This course in Health

Promotion was to prove an ideal preparation for what lay ahead. While I was in London, Peter was in Ireland looking after his elderly mother and was glad to have time with her after his many years away in Africa.

Women cannot speak when men are present

In 1995, during the month of May, I returned to Kenya and did my research for my thesis in Bura-Tana. This was the area in which I would work for the following ten years. When I went to do the research, I found willing helpers in the Maryknoll dispensaries, which I was to manage. All wanted to make an impression. You never know, the new boss might downsize! Everyone was most helpful, particularly the two Markyknoll sisters, Becky and Anastasia, from whom I was to take over the dispensaries.

I first trained the Maryknoll team and other helpers in the methodology of research, which was to be participative. 'Participation, Learning for Action' (PLA) this is sometimes known as Participatory Rural Appraisal (PRA).

I decided to work with a number of villages and a few Orma homesteads known as 'Manyattas'. However, it was quickly evident that we would have to separate the Orma men from the women. This was because in the Orma tradition, women cannot speak when men are present. So, they were broken up into two groups in each village. We asked each group to make a map of their village in the sand. The men's village was very good. You could see the Mosque, the cemetery, the roads, the canals and fields. In the woman's map, there was no Mosque but there was a drinking bar. There was a river and trees for firewood and every hut had a kitchen. We discussed the results of the map making with the participants. We asked why the women had not mentioned the Mosque or the cemetery. *"There is no place for us in the mosque and we are too busy looking after the living rather than the dead"* they said.

In November 1995, we arrived back in Kenya and asked for the transport which had been promised. Peter was to be parish priest, while I would run the five dispensaries. We agreed from the start to help each other in our work. In the six years together, we never had an argument, as we used to say that it was difficult enough as it was.

However, when we went to set off on our journey, there was no vehicle available, so we found ourselves driving my fifteen year old-year old Toyota Corolla to Tana River. Bright and early one November morning in 1996, Peter and I prepared to set off for our new home. Some friends, Holy Rosary sisters, turned up to wish us 'God Speed'. They came bearing gifts that they insisted we put into our overloaded car. On arrival in Bura-Tana, we found that hidden among table linen and other gifts, they had sneaked a litre of Bailey's Irish Cream, which we welcomed.

Fr Tom at home in Village 6, Bura Tana

Fetching water from a dam

The Bura Irrigation Settlement Scheme. The land is flat, no hills for miles.

Fr. Peter Suttle takes advantage of some unexpected rain

Hudson Mwalogho, health worker, takes a water sample from Tulu's Well

El Niño: the Hirimani River floods and we are cut off for three months

Dance Group welcomes the Apostolic Nuncio and Bishop Paul

Médecins Sans Frontières come to help during clashes between the Orma and Pokomo tribes

Fr. Tim Hutton keeps a watch out for crocodiles as we collect water from the Tana River

An Orma Manyatta is a group of residential dwellings of nomadic pastoralists

The interior of an Orma hut which is built only by women led by the bride, who decorate the inside with colourfully woven mats. Small animals sleep under the bed. The future husband jumps on top of the dwelling to ensure that it is well built

The active retired group of dancers show us a dance commemorating the Mau Mau fight for freedom

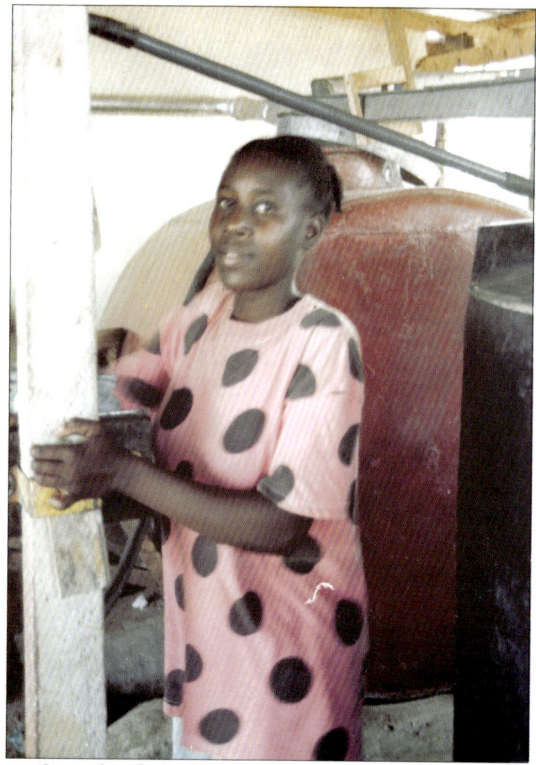
One of Lydia's daily tasks is pumping water up into the roof tank

Joseph Kamau, carpenter James Ngotho and uhuru Kenyatta with a silver-backed jackal which was trapped because it was attacking our poultry

All set for Mass in St. Mary's Church, Village 6. We later laid a new floor.

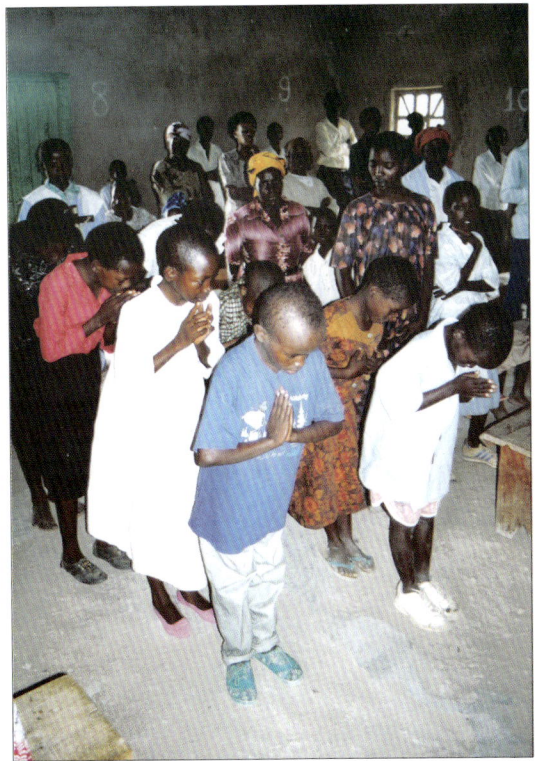

A dance troop lead the procession at Mass

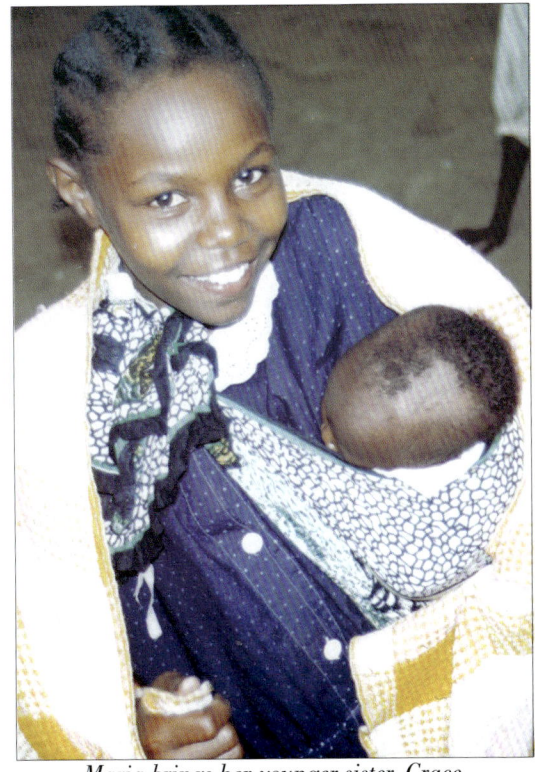

Maria brings her younger sister, Grace, to Mass on Sunday

Health worker, Nuru Kijana, uses simple methodology to demonstrate safe delivery in childbirth

Health worker, Nuru Kijana, uses simple methodology to demonstrate birthing problems

We are forced to burn food that had become contaminated

The residents of Village 6 repair the road so we can get relief supplies through

The first supply truck on the road after El Niño floods

Catholic Relief Services and Caritas Spain hire a plane to show us the extent of the Diocese of Garissa which is one sixth on the land mass of Kenya

Fr. Tim Hutton, Joseph Kamau, Bertie Gannon and Tom Hogan in a visit to Kamau's house

Orma dancers and Fr. Tom lead a dance and a song promoting better breast-feeding practices

Staff members, Rebecca and Lydia, enjoy our pumkin pie

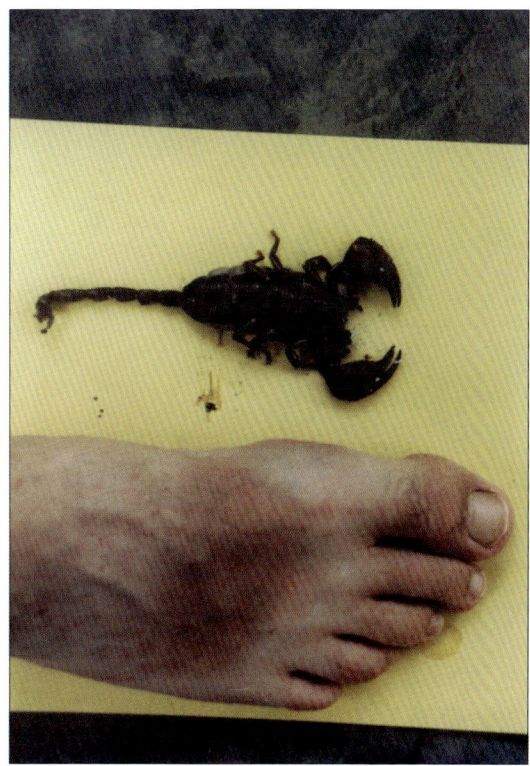

We always had to wear sandals in our home because of unwelcome visitors like this large scorpion beside my foot!

Our African rest house in our little garden at our home in Village 6

A baptism in S. Joseph's Church in Village 8

The people present a child to Fr. Tom and promise that they will look after her in his name and send her to school

Gathering water in preparation for drilling a well

A young boy and his donkey friend help transporting water to enable us drill for water

Mama Maria, gardener, and Mama Jane Mwai, cook, with Fr. Tom

Fr. Tom is made a member of the Orma tribe and does a little dance to celebrate

Meeting of health workers with Catholic Relief Staff

Head of the Parish Council presents Fr. Tom with a goat

My niece and God-child, Sinéad Phelan, comes to Bura-Tana and is married to Steven Clancy

Fr. Peter Suttle, Jane Mwai and Fr. Tom on their last day in Bura-Tana

New venture: Fr. Peter Ndegwa (centre) with staff who travel to Wenje to start a new parish

At Wenje we see the mighty Tana River

Cook Anna Wairimu in her kitchen and dining area at Br. Achuel's camp, Wenje

Our first toilet at our camp. Just whistle or sing when you are using it.

We immediately start mixing of concrete for block-making

Our first visitors to camp: Fr. Francis Thuku, Peter Ndegwa, Bishop Paul, Fr. Tom and Br. John

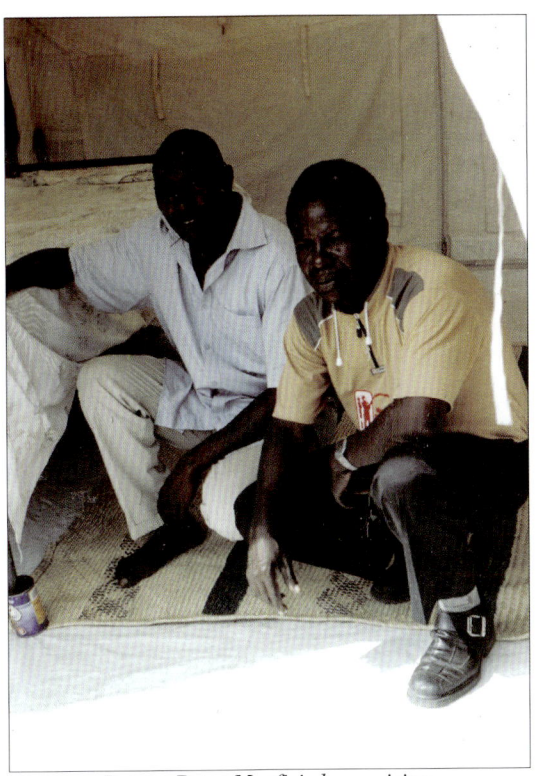

Driver, Peter Msafiri shows visitor, Hudson Mwalogho, our tented village

Cook Anna Wairimu shows visitor Lydia our tented accommodation

Frs. Peter Ndegwa, Dan Waweru and Tom get ready to launch our little boat

Our little boat in the mighty Tana River... my dog Brandy was taken by a crocodile while we were in the boat. We soon made plans for a larger boat!

Our youth group get ready to show us around the area

We travel to Thika for the ordination of Dan Waweru who has been posted to Wenje

Fr. Tom Hogan shows Fr. Pat Palmer, Irish Provincial, our new home

We dig a 'long drop' latrine

Seminarian, John Mujtisyha, shows us his tent

Members of the youth group show us how big one of the local trees is

Our power shower at our tented camp

Some of the local wildlife

Maria and seminarian, John Mujtisyha show us the dining room in our pre-fab house

Fr. Tom at his tented home in Wenje Parish in December 2005

Some of the local wildlife

Bura is an extraordinary place with wonderful people. I remember when I first went in 1995, being impressed by the faith of the tenant farmers – 'Simama Imara' was their favourite hymn – "Stand Firm in Your Faith". It is so true of these people. They had just spent two years without any resident priest. The Maryknoll Sisters used to come from Nairobi once a month to their former home in Village 6 and pay the dispensary staff and visit the Christians, catechists etc. At Easter and Christmas, they managed to get a student priest from Nairobi and got him up to Bura-Tana to officiate at the ceremonies. I seem to remember that they hired a bicycle taxi and that was how he got around from church to church.

Rain Harvesting, the Bura-Tana Mechanics Club and the 10 second shower

As soon as Peter and I set up our home in Village 6, we set about making the place as comfortable as possible. It was a simple, prefabricated, four bed roomed house, which had been transported from Nairobi on the back of a lorry. The wall panels were made of pressed straw, layered with cement and it was assembled in less than a week. The floors were cement and there was a little verandah at the back of the building which faced a small garden.

From the very start, it was clear that access to clean water was going to be one of our major problems in Bura–Tana. We knew that most patients attending one of our five dispensaries were suffering from water related diseases. We were told that water would be transported to us twice weekly by donkey cart. We would have to manage with four hundred liters – washing, cooking, drinking, and flushing the toilet! We did on occasion send the donkey cart out to the Tana River some nine kilometers away, to bring back some water. We also used the pick-up truck to transport water, but the river water was heavily polluted. We swore that if we ended up with no other source of drinking water, then we would have to abandon the place until such time as we could secure clean water. It was also important to have someone with you to act as look-out when you went to the river, because the Tana River is home to some large interesting crocodiles! The river water was used to flush the toilet in the house and for clothes washing. We had a supply of tablets which were meant to kill all the bacteria – we just hoped it would be safe enough for clothes washing. We had a rule about drinking water, which was to be boiled for twenty minutes and then filtered.

We decided that the first thing to do was to try and secure our water supply. In days past, water had been pumped by the Irrigation Scheme to a huge tank which overshadowed the village. However, it was dry all the time I was in Bura-Tana and water never ran from the taps in the villages.

There was a 'long drop' toilet built beside the house. We rebuilt the little cabin and put in a new cement slab. Peter used to call it his office! This meant that precious water would not be used to flush the toilet in the house, which used a septic tank.

We noticed that there were no rain gutters on the building and on our first morning in our new home, we found two locals to help us manufacture gutters out of some sheets of galvanized iron which we found lying near the house. I noticed two empty 200 litre drums in the church in Village 3. The Church elders kindly agreed to lend them to me. I had them repaired by the local blacksmith Hassan who was a very skilled man using charcoal, a bellows and a hammer to manufacture or repair all types of things. The two barrels became our first rain storage tanks in Village 6.

On arrival, I started a mechanics club at our house. This was a youth group and they were to help us in many jobs over the years, particularly in digging cars out of the mud! Long after the mechanics course was finished and the club closed, the members would respond to an emergency. I noticed a three thousand liter tank at St Francis church in Village 8. The tank had a hole in it but I was sure it could be repaired. I asked Bishop Paul if we could take the tank for repair and then use it for rain harvesting. He laughed, saying 'You don't know the Bura-Tana weather. It hardly ever rains here'. However, from previous research, I knew that statistics showed Bura had an average rainfall of two hundred mms per year. This is not enough for even dry weather crops to flourish but I had the last laugh, because when I had finished installing tanks in Village 6 and in the church compound in the main village of Bura-Tana, thanks to the heavy rain fall during El Nino, we had 27,000 litres of rainwater!

My nephew Conor and his wife Denise gave me some funds to try and improve our living standards. We used the first instalment to purchase a ten thousand litre plastic tank, as access to sufficient safe water was a priority. We built a base for the tank at the gable end of St Mary's Church in Village 6 and thatched the roof to protect the tank from the sun. Fortunately, St Mary's is a large church and a couple of hours of heavy rain filled the tank. A school friend of mine, Fr Brendan Duggan, from Tournafulla, who had joined me while I was doing research in the area, managed to get me some funding to purchase two more rain tanks. This time we went for five thousand litre tanks, which we placed at our house.

I managed to get some more funding for plastic tanks and later three metal tanks, which we placed in the St Jude's church compound. Two of the tanks there were actually sections of a petrol tanker that I found abandoned behind the church. I asked Father Joe from Hola, who was an expert welder, to come and help me as I thought some sections of the tanker could be salvaged. How right I was, he quickly cut out two sections for me and that gave us two more rain tanks. You need to be resourceful in the remote part of Africa!

Whenever it rained heavily and the tanks began to over-flow, Peter and I would go to the over-flow and fill every pot or basin in our house. We used to say that the only containers we didn't fill were the egg cups!! One time, when everything was full, Peter decided that it would be a good time to wash his hair in the rain! I suppose, it is only when you do not have something that you miss it and realize its value.

Some years later, I was very pleased when bringing Fr John Fogarty, who was on visitation from our headquarters in Rome to meet some villagers and that he noticed rain gutters around a villager's hut which had been roofed with second hand corrugated iron sheets. On enquiry, he was told by Philip Owiti that he and other villagers were following our example – we taught by example.

However, we never forgot to be careful in our use of water and the first place to be careful is the bathroom. When showering, one got into the shower, turned on the water for a few seconds, turned it off, soaped up and then turned on the shower again. It was all over in seconds! I remember our amaze-ment when one visitor went into the shower and used up the whole tank! We had to start pumping again to get water up into the roof tank. When we ran short of water, we would stop washing our clothes. Peter and I would then use all of our clothes until they were all dirty. We would then start using them again and give them a second run before washing clothes. The Fashion Police would not be very popular in Bura-Tana!

The New Commandments:

Mama Jane Mwai was engaged to be our cook. She had been to secondary school for two years, could read English and was well able to cook all the traditional dishes. However, we wanted her to move on further from the traditional dishes and learn some international cuisine! Peter and I started teaching her all the dishes that we knew. We started with the Ten Commandments for the kitchen and wrote everything down in a copy book!

The New Ten Commandments

1. First, wash your hands before cooking.
2. All drinking water to be boiled for twenty minutes and filtered when cool.
3. All ice cubes to be made with boiled water.
4. Always use the pressure cooker when possible.
5. Make an accurate shopping list for the monthly supermarket trip to Nairobi.
6. Turn off the gas when not in use.
7. Use a charcoal burner when cooking large amounts of food.

Sorry, but I seem to have forgotten the rest of the commandments…

Mama Mwai went on to become a wonderful cook and good friend who could bake cakes, tarts and all types of excellent things. Being able to bake bread was very helpful as the local baker in the village only had two types

– bread or no bread! Mama Mwai was quite at ease with guests and would gently remind those who tried to walk around the house in their bare feet, that this practice was unwise in an area that had many poisonous snakes and lots of scorpions!

Child Survival – Tunza Mtoto

Catholic Relief Services are the development agency of the Bishops Conference of USA. They have worked in Kenya for many years. In 1995, they wrote up a project designed to help the poorest of the poor. They looked for two areas in Kenya in which to do this work. Garissa on the Eastern seaboard and Homa Bay on the western side of Kenya were chosen.

The project was called Tunza Mtoto – Care for the Child. I was identified as the manager of the project and was the first person employed. At maximum, we were thirty staff: Co-ordinator, secretary, accountant, nurses, water technicians, driver-mechanics and security officers.

There were a number of sections in the programme. These were Immunization, Access to Safe Water and Education. We were to train 200 'barefoot doctors', ordinary men and women who would be doctors to their own people. We were to improve the skills of 500 Traditional Birth Attendants. We had funding for ten years to do this job. We enabled 100 villages to succeed in sinking a well. When we came to the chronological end of the programme, I paid off the staff; our work was done, the education would ensure that the good work would continue.

Our first Christmas in Bura-Tana

Peter and I had now settled into our house and were trying to make ourselves as comfortable as possible in the circumstances. We arranged to celebrate Mass in the six churches in and around the irrigation scheme. In two of the churches, we would have Midnight Mass and on Christmas Day, we would each celebrate Mass in the other churches.

I suggested to Peter that we should buy some sweets to give to the children who came to Mass. He thought it was a good idea and we purchased some large packets of sweets. As we were giving them out to the children, we told them the sweets came from Santa Claus. All the adults also seemed to become children for those few minutes and the sweets were given to children of all ages. The following day, I heard some of the Christians saying *"Wasn't it very good of Father Charles, to remember us here in Bura-Tana and to send us the sweets after all the years since he has been here"'* It was then we realised that they had never heard of Santa Claus and we quickly changed our tune and gave ourselves the glory and said *"Peter and Tom had bought the sweets"*. It reminded me of Bob Geldof and Midge Ure's song 'Do They Know It's Christmas?'

A parcel from Ireland, garlic worms and The Liquorice Allsorts Cake

One day, the local post master arrived by bicycle at our house with great news *"A parcel has arrived from Ireland"* he announced. Great excitement! *"Where's the parcel?"* we asked. *"Oh in the post office, you will have to come into the post office and sign for it"* he replied. So I put his bicycle in the back of our pick up truck and we drove the five kilometers to Bura village. The parcel came from my niece Sheena and contained all kinds of interesting things – a book on basic Chinese cooking, some spools of film and a large packet of Liquorice Allsorts! We put the sweets into the fridge for another day and Mama Mwai was later to put the book to good use and added Chinese dishes to her repertoire.

Not long after, Fr Sean McGovern, our new leader in Kenya, was to pay a visit. I alerted Mama Mwai that 'the big man' was coming and we should try and make a really good impression. She decided to cook a leg of goat and bake a cake. I reminded her that my sister, Helena, recommended making a few incisions in the leg of goat and inserting a few cloves of garlic. That night, as I was cutting the meat under our one small solar light, I was alarmed to see worms popping out from the slices of meat that I was cutting! Imagine what the boss will say! Fortunately, it was so dark Sean could not see too much. On enquiry from Mama Mwai, I was told that she had inserted a few cloves of garlic as requested in the meal – twenty cloves of garlic were used! It was great, and from then on, we always had a leg of goat with twenty cloves of garlic! So it was the garlic popping out of the meat and not worms as I had feared.

Mama Mwai had made a chocolate cake for the second course. Just before she put it into the oven, she had decided to smarten it up by sinking some of our precious Liquorice Allsorts into the top of the cake. The cake eventually arrived at our table. The liquorice was literally all sorts. It dribbled down the sides of the cake – it looked a terrible mess but it was a great cake and tasted wonderful!

God sends us a hunter

One morning, a man arrived at my door. Mama Mwai said *"God has sent a hunter, and he has a leg of goat to sell"*. I went outside and had a look at the leg of goat which was concealed in a sack – the leg of goat was a piece of ostrich! I purchased the leg of 'goat' and asked Mama Mwai how should we cook the ostrich. She said *"There are three ways to cook ostrich"*. We started off the first night with recipe number one and the second night we went for recipe number two – we got no further – goujons of ostrich and chips. From then on, the odd time a poacher came to my house with a leg of 'goat' it was recipe number two that was used. I asked Mama Mwai where she had got the recipes and she reminded me that I had given her a present at Christmas time of a book on game cooking.

We had few visitors to Bura-Tana. This was because one had to come by military convoy and there was also a curfew from 7 p.m. to 6 a.m. However, visitors who did arrive were encouraged to share their culinary skills with Mama Mwai. A group of Korean Missionaries began working with the Diocese in sinking wells. One day, they arrived with a large group of young Koreans. No English was spoken except by their leader who was fairly fluent. The ladies befriended Mama Mwai and they cooked using only the language that cooks use! From then on, Mama Mwai always used a pressure cooker to do rice and could make dishes using the plentiful supply of dried seaweed which our visitors brought us.

We always prided ourselves on our table. It was the only and best restaurant around. I had come with a set of Waterford Crystal glasses, which I received as an ordination present from some primary school friends in Tramore. Tommy Kavanagh and Teddy O'Connor said *'You can have this Waterford Glass but you must promise us that it will travel with you where ever you go!'* I have kept that promise and now the glasses have returned to Ireland after a 31 year stay in Africa. Some one asked Peter what he brought to the house "Myself", he said. They kindly gave him a tablecloth of Irish Linen.

Mama Helen learned how to use starch on the linen cloth so it looked its best. With a few candles on the table, some wild flowers, the cloth and the glasses, the setting looked just magical. Peter used to say that he had never been so well fed. However, when you live five hundred kilometres from the nearest supermarket, you learn to shop wisely and you only forget an item once – remember our 5th Commandment!

Over the years, our collection of cook books expanded, from the simple Elizabeth Zani's 'Mpishi Ya Kisasa' (Today's Cook) to Huisgenoot (Good Housekeeping) from South Africa. The South African cookbooks were especially useful as they used all the African vegetables.

Here is our recipe for Stuffed Pumpkin which was the dish most requested at our table.

Ingredients:
One pumpkin.
Cooked rice – amount depends on the size of the pumpkin.
Two table spoons of ground nutmeg.
A fist-full of breadcrumbs.
500 gms of minced meat.
300 mls of chicken stock.
4 cloves of garlic.
2 onions.

Method:
Cut the top off of the pumpkin and keep aside.
Remove seeds and stringy bits from inside the pumpkin.
Rub salt on the inside of the pumpkin.

Stuffing:
Fry the minced meat in a little olive oil in a pan.
Add 2 tablespoons of nutmeg.

Add the onions and garlic.
Add the chicken stock.
Add in the rice and bread crumbs.
Now stuff the pumpkin with the mixture.
Rub olive oil on the pumpkin.
Put the lid back on and fix with tooth picks.
Cook in the oven at 180 degrees for 45 mins or so.

Serve directly on the table: your guests will be surprised and wonder where you got the lovely container for the meal, because the pumpkin will looks like a piece of pottery! The flesh of the pumpkin is your vegetable for the meal. Anything left over will make a good base for tomorrow's soup! I still cook this recipe now that I'm back in Ireland and it goes down a treat.

Impregnated Nets

The Maryknoll Sisters had developed five dispensaries in Bura-Tana. These were dotted around the scheme and allowed villagers easy access to health care. I was the director of the dispensaries for nine years.

One third of all patients who presented themselves at Maryknoll dispensaries had symptoms of malaria. It was very common in the area and a particularly virulent form was cerebral malaria. Over the years, we made efforts at prevention, mainly by encouraging people to use mosquito nets impregnated with insecticide. The nets were known as 'Impregnated Nets'. However, we were forced to change the name as parents would not cover their daughters with the impregnated nets – *"Oh I couldn't have my daughter sleeping in that, she might become pregnant"* one man told me. Thus our nets were renamed as Insecticide Treated Nets.

A coffin made from doors

Shortly after our arrival in Bura-Tana, Margaret, the administrator of Maryknoll Dispensaries, came to say that we would have to intervene in the care of a sick young boy. He had been attending our facility and had been diagnosed with malaria and given medicine. He had been vomiting and had diarrhoea for some days and was not improving. I went and found him with his ten-year-old brother in a little house. Their parents were not working in the area and the boys were looking after the house, while they also went to school. Our young patient was already unconscious when we put him into the back of the small Toyota Station wagon and set off for the Health Centre. On arrival, we carried him onto the corridor and laid him down on the cement floor. The nurse came and started attending to him. I was shocked when I heard the nurse say to me *"This one has gone"*.

There was nothing for it but to go back to the village with the dead body. In a few minutes, our Toyota station wagon changed from its role as ambulance to that of a hearse. When we got to the village, I went to the ten-year-old. I told him how sorry I was to have to say that his brother has just died. I was later to find out that this sixteen year old youth was actually twenty four years of age. However, he did not wish to shame himself and reveal his real age as he was still in primary school.

Preparations went ahead immediately for the funeral. Messengers were sent by bus to call the parents from the far off town where they were working. A hole was dug in the floor of the hut and the body laid into it and packed around with wet sand. This was the local method of preserving bodies. This was our first time meeting James Ngotho, the local carpenter who also seemed to double as the one to lay out bodies. We later were to meet him in his role as the local pathologist. It was he who removed the dead foetus of a woman who had died. Tradition had it that the mother and the child in the womb had to be buried separately.

However, on this occasion, he was making the coffin out of two doors from someone else's house. Peter and I were shocked at this situation and remarked to each other that we had never met such poor people. This was real poverty, like we had never seen before.

The funeral day arrived and those preparing the body for burial finished their work and the coffin was sealed, after the whole village had had a good look at our young man. I then heard a request for soap so that those who had been handing the body could wash. Eventually, from one house, a tiny piece of soap was found.

There was a delay as we waited for some guests to arrive and I took the opportunity to go into the nearby village to buy some provisions. I bought some planks of wood, vegetables and was lucky to be able to buy a crate of beer. I arrived back just in time for the funeral Mass and so had no time to unload the car. At the end of the ceremony, the head man spoke and asked parents not to go away from the village leaving children unattended. When the mother of the dead child got her turn to speak, she asked people not to interfere in her private life. The people were not impressed and told her so.

The time came for the final journey. We were just about to go to the little graveyard with the coffin. I was taken aback to hear the head man saying "*Fr Tom will help us with the car and we will all follow behind*". I thought of the luggage in the car – the crate of beer! – it is not so easy to hide! Hurriedly I went to the car, did my best to camouflage the crate of beer, the cabbages and potatoes. The coffin just about squeezed in. However, no one made any comment nor showed surprise. We got our fiftieth puncture on that journey. Later on, we replaced the new tyres with sixteen ply tyres, which were not so prone to punctures.

The Kibiriti kit
– health in a match box

The Kibiriti kit was simply a match box filled with all that you need when delivering a baby. Through our dispensaries, we urged pregnant women to prepare a Kibiriti Kit – a simple match box filled with a new razor blade, a small piece of soap and two pieces of string which has been boiled and some cotton wool. Attached to the box with an elastic band was a packet with a pair of surgical gloves. These items would be used by the Traditional Birth Attendant when the time came for the pregnant women to deliver. It was a simple way of promoting more hygienic deliveries. The Birth Attendants, who were unlettered, kept a record of births using maize and beans. A live birth meant that you put one kernel of maize in a jar, but you use a red kidney bean for infants who died. It was a simple but effective method of keeping track of the live birth rate.

During one of these meetings, my staff and I were explaining something that we had learned during the Lactating Specialists Course which we had attended. We had been told that if the after-birth cannot be expelled by the mother, the baby must be put to the breast and the contractions will start again. The TBAs were not impressed because in Orma culture, babies are not put to the breast until two days after birth. The mother is given a rest and no value is seen in the colostrum first produced by a woman. 'It's just water' they said. Instead, babies are given milk of the cow since Orma call themselves *'People of the Cow'*.

However, we had made our point and forgot about it until the following month, when one of the women explained that she had dealt with a most difficult case during the previous week. She explained that the young mother could not expel the afterbirth, so the TBA remembered what we had said at the meeting and she put the baby to the breast. The afterbirth was expelled after a short time. We needed to say no more. The message was spread like wild fire throughout the district. One of our own TBAs had become our best teacher!

Merry Go Round

We organized a monthly meeting for the TBAs. This occasion was used to increase their knowledge and to discuss problems that they had faced during the previous month. To ensure their presence, we also ran a financial 'Merry Go Round'. Every month, each woman would put five shillings, about one euro) into the pot and one name would be picked out. She would then receive all the money collected that month. Eventually, each one had had their month and we started the second round. However, there was a problem with the title 'Merry go Round'. I didn't understand this until I was told that some of the women did not like the name 'Mary Go Round' because of its Christian links. I assured them that this had nothing to do with Mary, the Mother of God.

Female genital mutilation (FGM) is outlawed in Kenya. However, in our district it was widely practiced and in the Orma culture, 98% of females received the most severe form of circumcision which is known as infibulation. In this operation, the girl is circumcised and then stitched up. It brought huge problems for women, when they were girls, adults and finally as older women. Now it was because of our regular contact with the TBAs that we found out the great secret! It turned out that some of our TBAs were also practicing as circumcisers. There was little we could do to change this and we often said that this custom will only be stopped by women themselves. When we did speak about it, the men said they had nothing to do with it. However, we found out that it was the men who paid for the operation and also that they would not marry an uncircumcised woman – so they had a lot to do with the custom.

A letter from Al Qaida

We once received a threatening letter, purporting to be from Al Qaida. I had to go to the police and also to Catholic Relief Services for advice on the matter. The security consultant for Catholic Relief Services recommended that we increase our security and funds were made available for this. The police recommended keeping our travel plans secret, changing our travel routes in the area and varying travel times. I gave our driver mechanics strict instruction to be back at base before sundown and to make no exceptions. Whoever wrote the letter knew us and was able to say that my deputy was a Luo woman.

I knew that it was very important for me to remain cool, calm and collected. As leader, I knew it was vital that I showed no fear – however, inevitably it caused stress to us all.

Can crocodiles see in the dark?

It was in Bura-Tana that I first learned about coping mechanisms – actions that families take to exist in difficult times. It was one July, during a food security survey, that I acted as interpreter for a doctor from Medecins sans Frontiers. The doctor asked Mama Victoria, whom I knew very well, many questions – family size, crops in the fields, possible sources of income and so on. Mama Victoria was well able to answer the questions and we were all feeling very comfortable when gently he asked *'And when did you last eat meat?'* Victoria said to me "Fada Tom, this is very embarrassing". I suggested that if we tell the truth, Medecins sans Frontier might be able to help us. So she replied and said *"We slaughtered one of our four chickens last Christmas"* So for six months, Mama Victoria's family of five people had not had any meat at all! It showed just what tough times the people lived in.

When times really got tough in Taita and people's backs were to the wall, the Wataita would eat their maize seed for the following year. This was a sign of their desperation. However, these people in Bura-Tana would go and collect all the bones of dead animals that they could find. The bones were then sold by the lorry load and transported to Nairobi where the bones were ground up for animal feed.

I noticed that the Orma, who are semi-nomadic, would not wait for a cow that went down when they were moving herds for fresh grass. Now and then, you would see a cow down by the edge of the road. The sick cow would be left for the lions and hyenas.

One time, when I was in the Wenje area where the Pokomo tribe live, my staff and I were to cross the Tana River and visit a government run medical clinic. Some of the staff would not cross by canoe for fear of crocodiles. Three of us hired a canoe and a boatman and crossed and walked the long distance to the clinic. I noticed that our boatman made sure to make a lot of noise and frequently bashed his paddle 'accidentally' off the side of the canoe! I was later to learn that this is a good way to keep crocodiles at bay. It took us longer to reach the dispensary and so we were delayed on our return journey. I was having difficulty in keeping up, so I met a man with a bicycle and hired him and his bicycle to transport me. It was pitch black when we returned in the evening and called out for our boat man who came across the river to fetch us. I remember the conversation well *"Can crocodiles see in the dark?"*

We arrived safely and then heard from our colleagues that while they were waiting for us, they noticed that no efforts were being made by the women to prepare an evening meal. On enquiry, the villagers told them that in difficult times the families only ate one meal at lunch time each day. Fortunately, we were able to arrange a ''Food for Work Programme' which helped them. We made arrangements for the sick and elderly that other villagers would work in their name. Children were also encouraged to go to school as this was recorded as their work.

Dedeche

One day I was called to a meeting with the Orma elders and was very pleased to learn that I was going to be made a member of the tribe. The elders ground coffee beans and the resulting oil was used to anoint my forehead. The name given was 'Dedeche' which is a name of a tree in the area, the tree under which people gather and meet. When giving my name, I was told to say *"My name is Dedeche from Hirimani"*. It was a great honour to be made a member of the tribe.

El Niño

El Niño occurred in 1999 in Bura Tana. Heavy rains fell in many parts of the world and our Village 6 in Bura Tana was no exception. Our normal annual rainfall of two hundred mm fell in two days and the mighty Tana River began to flood more than usual and then its tributaries began to flood. Just beside the village, the seasonal river got higher and higher. The Irish bridge which we used to cross the normally dry river bed became impassable. With an Irish bridge, a cement road runs down the river bank across the river bed and up the far side – you can cross the river when the water is not over the front wheels of your truck!

The river got higher and higher and no vehicle could cross. In fact, the road was impassable long before you met the river. One night, we heard whistles being blown in the village and the village crier began to shout in his high pitched voice and called all the men to come out of their homes. The village head man came to say that the river was breaking its banks and the dyke that protected the village from flooding was under threat. He said *"The river is eating into the dyke and if we don't do something we are all going to be flooded"*

Now, in the Church store, we had lots of empty sacks which had been used to transport food supplements for the people as there had been a hunger going on at that time. The men were out all night from 2 a.m. to early morning, bagging and filling the bags with soil or sand to hold the embankment, so that we would not be flooded. After putting the few valuables we had on our dining table and the medicines from the medical store up on shelves, we went to see the dyke. The speed and power of the water was frightening. The local cemetery was flooded, and we saw various corpses and a coffin or two being swept down the river, all the way to Mombasa. It was a difficult time for us all.

I remember once, a young man from the village tried to cross the river. He had his bicycle, so he tied the bicycle around his shoulders and had a strap across his forehead. He said he would walk through the river as far as he could and then go under the water a little bit and then come up the far side. Of course, he never succeeded and we were involved in the search for the body. James Ngotho of my staff, who had previously worked with the Kenya Police forces in water rescue, managed to find the body. He brought it up and we dragged it to the road, where it had to remain until the police came and told us what to do with the body. They did not come for two days and in that tremendous heat, the body began to swell. James Ngotho, however, knew how to release the excess gases in the body, simply by putting a bicycle spoke through the stomach. Since the local cemetery was flooded, his family buried him in the bush in a shallow grave. He did not happen to be a member of our church, or any church for that matter and no prayers were said over him. No ceremony of any kind. He had been a young man who had got heavily involved in drugs. It was all very sad.

For a couple of months, we were cut off from the main village, but I was able to get out onto the tarmac road to Garissa, by using a 4x4 vehicle. With my foot to the floor and driving in first or second gear, I was able to plough through the thick mud and get on the tarmac road.

One time on a journey, Peter Suttle

said to me, *"Try and get some fresh meat"*. On the way to Garissa, I saw a woman selling some chickens which I bought and thought *"That's a good idea. I'll buy all the chickens from her and we can slaughter them when when required"*. I bought the half dozen chickens and brought them back to our compound, where we began to look after them. After a day or two, one or two of them began to lay eggs. *"This is great; we are going to get eggs now"*. So, from then on, we raised chickens. Of course, to have laying hens in that area you have to have a cock and duly our cock was purchased and called 'Sportsman'. Sportsman Number One served his time and was duly eaten and then we had Sportsman Number Two – I never did get around to eating him as he was spared after all the good work.

The Somali

The Somali tribe live in a number of countries – Ethiopia, Kenya and Somalia. They are a proud warrior people. There are twelve clans among Somali people. Clan balance is a very contentious issue, as there are frequent faction fights between the clans.

At one time, the Diocese of Garissa was considering doing some health work in North Eastern Kenya. This did not happen, mainly because of the problems that we saw other agencies facing when working there. We met one British agency, who aimed at working with children. For three months, they hung around their office and a barn storage facility full of food, unable to work because of difficulties as regards clan-balance. Employment regulations in the agency meant that you had to employ the best person for the job. The local elders wanted the agency to employ people purely on a clan-balance basis. This was not possible and the agency eventually was forced to withdraw and did not do any of the work which had been planned.

We eventually decided that we would have more success with the Somali in the area of animal health. We had seen the great respect that they gave to their animal herds and were aware that animal health was frequently given more emphasis than human health, particularly the health of girls. In times of illness, it was more likely for an animal to get medicine than a girl. Unfortunately we did not manage to get funding for such a project and the situation remains the same at this time.

Educating Lucy

One Christmas, some young teenage girls arrived at my house carrying twenty kilos of maize on their heads. They gave me the maize and some little money. Lucy, who was their leader, told me that they were members of the Holy Childhood Association and that they had gone carol singing as the Star Singers. They had dressed up as the Three Wise Men, made a star from cardboard and silver paper and one of them dressed as an angel to carry it. One evening, they went carol singing to the seven catholic homes in Village 3.

On their way to nearby Village 4, some older boys threw stones at them. I later found out that these were Muslim boys. The choir returned home and got some of the elders to escort them and finished their mission. One farmer gave them the maize in gratitude for a good harvest.

The following morning they walked the four kilometres to my house and told me that the gifts were for children who were worse off than they were. I promised them that I would match their efforts and find a child in need.

That very evening, a lady came to my house upset that there was nothing in her hut to feed her children. I told her she was in luck and that six children of the parish had gone carol singing and had collected some food and money. I made an offer to the lady of some casual labour for the following week and gave her an advance. She went off a happy woman, with the maize on her head and her arms loaded with vegetables and cooking oil.

The generosity of these girls really struck me. My work in the area of health meant that I was aware of the girls' health status. These were children who had all gone through various stages of malnutrition themselves. Most of them had stunted growth, yet here they were trying to help other children.

From research in the Tana River, we knew that if a girl went to primary school, even for a few years, it had a dramatic effect on the health of her children. She will have fewer children and they will be fully immunized, better nourished and better educated.

I resolved to try and do something for these girls and get them into secondary school. Recent research has shown that girls who are educated improve the local economy. When I was on sick leave in Ireland, I took the opportunity to speak about the girls' generosity and I succeeded in getting sufficient money to help them each buy a small herd of goats. These herds would enable them to have school fees for the future. They are all in different secondary schools at the time of writing.

Stick your thumb in the crocodile's eye!

There are lots of crocodiles in the Tana River – big crocodiles. We often saw them when we went to collect water at the river, as someone always had to keep watch. One quiet Sunday afternoon, some villagers came to my home, bringing me the message that a schoolboy named Hassan had been attacked by a crocodile on the far side of the river and was being transported by canoe and then by donkey cart to the Mission compound. As soon as I saw him, I knew it was clear from the deep wound and the visible bone in his broken shoulder that hospitalisation would be required.

We managed to staunch the bleeding and decided to transport him by jeep to the Provincial Hospital in Garissa. Knowing that I would be travelling during the hours of curfew, I went to the police station and asked the inspector for a police escort. He called two of his officers and checked their supply of ammunition before departure. We set off on our journey, being careful not to give the boy anything to drink, even though he kept on asking for water. I would just wet his lips as I knew that an operation would surely have to take place, provided I could find a surgeon.

I entered the hospital on that Sunday evening and asked the policemen to stay close by me. A European with an armed escort in a hospital makes a big impression! I must have looked like a very important person, as everyone ran round and seemed anxious to help. I was soon directed to two Norwegian doctors from the Rotary Club. The doctors had just come out of the operating theatre, where they had treated a Somali man with bullet wounds. Dr Johan and his wife, who was also a surgeon, said they must operate immediately. Our young man was soon in the operating theatre and eventually he recovered.

Sometime later, Hassan told us what had actually happened that Sunday morning. He had been watering his father's cows in the river and afterwards he had gone into the river for a wash. Suddenly, a crocodile attacked him and knocked him down. He thought that he was finished, but just before he was dragged under the water he stuck his thumb in the crocodile's eye. The croc released his grip and the boy escaped. He sat for his primary school examination soon after, writing with his left hand of course. Surely his essay was the most interesting one in the examination. So if a crocodile ever catches you, remember to stick your thumb in the crocodile's eye!

The Christmas Crib

Rains fell during one September and it was a difficult month because of all the mud. I was tired by the end of the month. Michael, my friend contacted me and said *"You need a holiday and we are going to go to Rome. Why not contact your friend Fr Eddie O'Farrell there and see if we can get accommodation in your Mother House in Italy?"*

So I went to Rome and enjoyed a most interesting time. I was very impressed when Eddie even arranged an audience with Pope John Paul.

While I was wandering around the city doing some shopping, I was enthralled with some Christmas Cribs that I came across. The cribs had beautifully carved figures. 'Wouldn't it be wonderful to bring one crib back home to Bura-Tana. The people would be very pleased', I thought. However, when I looked at the price of a crib, I decided that my money could be better spent on the people of my village.

All too soon it was time to leave. I went to the Bursar of our house and asked for my account. *"Father Tom, please, there is no account. You are a house holder, haven't you paid a small tax each year to help us run this house?"* And indeed, I had always paid the small tax that was requested each year. It felt very good to be told that I was a house holder.

I returned just in time for the busy Christmas ministry and had an easy time with the Christmas Sermon. I just told the Christians of my visit to Rome and how I had met the Pope. He had even told me to bring his special blessings to the people and particularly the sick and the children. Needless to say, the people did not quite know what an 'Audience' with the Pope meant and they thought that I had had a one to one meeting with the man himself. In each of the six churches, they gave Pope John Paul a great round of applause. In St Jude's Church, the catechist said *'The Holy Father knows Father Tom and John Paul knows about us here in Bura-Tana and told Father Tom to bring us his blessings. Isn't it wonderful?'* I did not have the heart to explain that I had met Pope John Paul in the great Hall with thousands of other people! The news that I had met the Pope went round the villages so quickly I chose not to try and explain too much!

When I arrived in Village 2 for Midnight Mass, the choir were in full voice. I could hear the drums throbbing as I drove through the empty cotton fields. Mama Rosa, the chairlady, met me on arrival and helped set up a cable to the church, running from the car battery of my truck. This would give us power to light one forty watt bulb and it would be our only light for the celebration.

But we had plenty of candles, so the whole place looked lovely with the candles flickering.

Just before the service began, Mama Rose then brought me to see the Christmas Crib. I could just see the gleam in her eye and how proud she was of the children's Crib which was lit by a bicycle lamp. She explained that she had gathered all the children during the school holidays and the children had made all the figures for the crib out of mud and had dried the figures in the blazing hot sun. How glad I was, that I had not brought home a crib from Rome! The simple crib in Village 2 was the best crib ever.

Dead woman in my jeep

Peter used to visit the sick regularly and one evening he told me of a friend of ours who was seriously ill. Her one wish was to be brought home to her village in Ukambani District before she died. Peter promised to fulfil her death wish. It just happened that I had to travel to Nairobi for a hospital appointment that very week. Would there be room in my Land cruiser for the sick woman and a friend? Of course I agreed, for a promise made is a debt unpaid.

Early one bright morning, we set off to get the woman from her hut. I was surprised to see that she had to be carried to the truck, as we had not realised just how ill she was. It is a long journey to Ukambani, and takes about four hours. We were well into the journey when the minder said *'This woman has left this world'*. I stopped the car, quickly checked for a pulse or heart beat, but there was no sign of life. She was dead. Now to travel in Kenya with a dead body, you need a number of documents, one being a death certificate. There was no time for such matters, so I left the woman seated in her car seat, tied the seat belt up good and tight and put a white veil over her face. For a woman who was dead she was not looking too bad! On we went and sure enough, just after a rise on the road, we came upon a police check point. When the police stopped our car for a routine check, I remembered what my Uncle, 'Jumbo' Cooper a navy veteran, used to say *"Always promote an officer by one rank and if you are not sure you can always address him as Inspector. Sergeant"*, I said *"Mother is not so well and we are bringing her home to her parents"*. The police wished us God speed and we continued on our journey.

As we approached the woman's home village, I suggested to Peter that he should go ahead on foot and talk to the parents. If we were to arrive in the homestead with a dead body in the car, all hell would break loose. People would start weeping and wailing. I parked the car under the shade of a mango tree and Peter and the minder went ahead. Not long after, some curious onlookers arrived. I saw them looking at the luggage in my jeep, including my silent passenger. It was not long before they asked me about the lady who was sitting so quietly in the car. I told them gently that the lady had died on the journey, as we were bringing her home to her village and to her parents. The people were very kind to me and gave me some ripe mangoes to refresh me as I waited for Peter.

Sometime later, Peter returned and we drove slowly to the homestead. People were very calm. The family thanked us for bringing their daughter home. What a homecoming…

Now, matters were not yet finalised. We still had no death certificate and no burial certificate. I was due to be admitted to hospital that night for a check up and we simply had to continue on our journey. So, we went to a friend, Fr Paul Chua, who just happened to be the local parish priest. He was very helpful and sent us on our way, assuring us that the necessary requirements would be attended to and the obsequies would be held for our friend.

The cabbage that became a flower

The diocese of Garissa is the largest in Kenya and covers one sixth of its landmass. Once, Caritas Spain and CRS jointly hired a plane and brought eight of us to fly over the area, to see just how far the Diocese extended. We were to fly from Nairobi and Peter Suttle suggested that I bring some goods like fruit and vegetables with me, as we were going to visit some missionaries who worked in an area even more remote than ours. I went to the supermarket in Nairobi and stocked up on supplies. The following morning we all met in Wilson Airport and were weighed together with our luggage, before we entered the plane. Fortunately, one of our passengers failed to show up and this gave me the opportunity to put seventy kilos of the goodies on board. One of my cardboard boxes was too large to fit in the small hold of the plane, so I just stuffed cabbages under any seat I could find. As we took off, one or two of the cabbages went flying down the aisle. It was going to be an interesting journey.

We landed in El Wak and were met by two Italian sisters who lived there in very simple conditions – they had seventeen Catholics who used to meet weekly in their house, which had to double as a home, clinic and church. I arrived with some gifts for the sisters – some dried garlic, a few tins of tomato paste and some vegetables. Just before we flew off to Mandera, I asked one of the Sisters if I had given them a cabbage that I had brought for them. I was told that I hadn't, so I looked in the plane and found two under the seats. I handed sister the cabbage and said 'I'm sorry that I don't have a bunch of flowers for you' she replied *"To us this is a bouquet of flowers"*. So the cabbage had become a flower.

We flew to Wajir and celebrated Mass with the Christians there. The previous year, some angry Muslims had ransacked their church. The crucifix had been damaged and the figure of the Christ broken. They had repaired the church but left the broken cross as a memory. So I told them the following story. During the Korean War, US soldiers were advancing on an enemy position – a barrage of shells had softened it up. As they made their way through the dust, they were surprised to come upon a church and were sad to see that they had caused serious structural damage. Even the statue of the cross outside the building had lost its hands. They were even more surprised when, out of the rubble, a small figure emerged. It was the local priest. They were sorry, they said, for the damage caused but they would be able to help repair the statue of the Christ. Now new arms could be made and attached to the statue and it would be as good as new. *"No"* said the priest, *"let us leave it as it is and instead put a sign at the foot saying 'I have no hands, you are my hands'"*.

Visitors at night

I was awoken one night by Nicholas, our watchman, running noisily outside the house and shouting in Kiswahili *'Beware, beware, there is trouble'*. As he ran along, I could hear his Wellington boots go 'clump clump'. I got up and wrapped a towel around me and checked that Peter was also awake. I knew something was about to happen. Voices could be heard outside our compound gate. We opened the door and stepped onto the veranda. *"Who are you and what do you want?"* we shouted. In reply, they used Peter's African pet name 'Mtua', so obviously they knew us. They told us that they had someone very sick and we shouted back *"Where is the headman from the village?"* It had been arranged with the elders, that we were never to open our door at night to anyone unless accompanied by the watchman and the village headman. Next moment, I saw a flash and saw the outline of a gun with a banana shaped magazine – an AK 47. We were in trouble. As they broke down the garden gate, I slammed the door. We grabbed our emergency whistle and began blowing as hard as we could. We had previously distributed two other whistles in the village and hoped that others would also start blowing to sound the alarm. I suggested to Peter that we escape by the back door, but he said that he thought there was someone at the back of the house. I then asked him to climb up in the attic of the house with me – I felt sure that our intruders would never think of someone up above the ceiling. Peter was reluctant and said that he would meet them as he grabbed a large 20mm spanner. I said *"They have guns, Peter"* He was stubborn and said he would wait to meet them. I felt that I had to stay with him. So we stayed and awaited our fate; we decided to hide inside the house and I went into one of the bathrooms and hid under a washbasin – I didn't feel so hidden!

There was dead silence for a while and suddenly the main door broke open with a crash – then more silence. I could hear them coming and soon they found Peter and began questioning him, asking for money. They began to beat him brutally with sticks. I could hear the swish of the sticks as they were brought down on him. I can still hear the swish of the sticks now and Peter's groans as each thump hit him. His cries became fainter as the beating proceeded. He began to pray and I heard him say the Act of Contrition. I knew that I would be next.

My heart was pounding in my chest – I thought it would burst. Sure enough, I could hear one of the intruders edging nearer and nearer. Ever so slowly, the door of the bathroom opened, a dim torch swept the room and then the beam fixed on me. I was roughly grabbed and brought out to meet the head robber. He shoved his rifle into my stomach and said *"You know what this is; you know what it is for?"* he said. He asked for money, and I asked where they had put Peter, who was now silent. One began to beat me with his walking stick. I kept going closer to him so that he would not be able to get a good swing at me. *"Why are you beating me, what do you want?"* I asked. They said they wanted money, *"I have money"*, I told them and led them to my bedroom. I handed over my staff salaries for the month and hoped that the bandits would leave. They told me to get the keys of the car – I took the keys of the old pick-up and handed them over – *"No, you are going to drive"* they said. *"I am not driving anywhere without some clothes, my glasses and my shirt and hat"*. I knew that they would abandon me way out in the bush and that I would be in the burning sun for the day. I was very uneasy, my heart was pounding. I feared for my life and was unsure whether Peter was still alive. They frog-marched me to the door. Suddenly, a loud shot rang out and bullets began to fly. My attackers fired a few rounds and suddenly they fled away. I was alone on the veranda. I entered the house and looked for Peter, I found him eventually, lying on the floor of the visitors' room. There was lots of blood. We held each other and waited and waited. It took us some time before we realised that the bandits had left. We heard a voice outside – Saidi, the home guard from Village 5 had turned up, I saw him on the veranda holding his World War 1 vintage Lee Enfield rifle at the ready. He told us that our watchman had run down to his village and told him that robbers were attacking the Fathers' house. It turned out that many of the villagers had heard the shots and the shouting. They had hurled stones up on the tin roof of the little Community hall in the hope that the bandits might flee. However, I have no memory of that sound. Saidi said he would stay on guard all night with Nicholas our watchman.

It was a long, long night and sleep did not come easily. Morning broke. Nuru Kijana, our nurse came to the door, asking if she could help. We both had a look at Peter. There was lots of blood, but we could not see a wound. We stripped him down and put him into the shower - then we could see that he was bleeding from the buttocks. He had been stabbed in order to make him confess as to where his money was. However, Peter was stubborn and would not give the bandits anything.

I drove him into the little town of Bura, where there was a half-baked Sudanese medic who ran a clinic. He had a look at the wound and agreed with our prognosis that Peter would have to be stitched. In his kindness, he would not let us pay anything for the treatment. On our return to our house, we found that many of the locals had come and encamped themselves on our veranda. They brought benches from the church and stayed the whole day and were a great comfort to us. They were made welcome by Mama Jane Mwai our cook, as Peter and I could barely function, but our reliable cook realised our duty of hospitality to visitors and helped the people in preparing lots of hot tea. There were quiet hymns and prayers and as the morning went on, our visitors asked us to join them on the veranda where they prayed with us. It was a good lesson to us.

The Bishop and Vicar General of the Diocese heard the news and rushed to be with us. The leader of Catholic Relief Service (CRS) with whom I worked, rang to say he would charter a plane and fly us out and that CRS would provide counselling as necessary. However, we said that we did not think that this was necessary, but we would talk about the event between ourselves, which indeed we did for many a night. Our leader in Kenya, Fr Larry Shine, arrived the following morning and suggested that we take some time off. We decided to stay at our post for a week or more and then take a rest. Peter and I subsequently received counselling to help us deal with the traumatic event of that night. This was the first of a number of attacks. Peter never felt comfortable again in Bura.

Some time later, I told him one day that the Police Inspector has just warned me of an impending attack. The police asked for permission to put armed men in the compound, in order to fight it out with the bandits *"We kill the bastards Padre"* as they said. Peter decided to leave the following morning and asked me if I would join him for Mass at 5 a.m. Later on that evening, I found him fuelling the pick-up vehicle. I asked what he was doing and he said *"See, judge and act"*. Bright and early the following morning, we celebrated Mass together, had a quick breakfast and packed his little luggage into the pick-up truck and left for Nairobi. He was appointed to parish work in St Austin's Nairobi. He left Kenya some years later and took up a new position in Gambia, West Africa. I continued on in Bura for the following six years.

Water, water everywhere and rain dams?

During the Child Survival Programme, we did a lot of work with water. We purchased two hand augurs, which could be used in the soft soil, within two kilometres of the Tana River. A hand held augur is a device which enables you to drill for water up to a depth of ten to twenty metres. We looked for villages who were interested in getting a supply of clean water. We would lend them the augur and a technician. The village had to supply all the man power to operate the augur. Ten strong people were needed to push the bars of the augur each day and the village would feed all those involved! We helped over one hundred villages gain access to clean water. One village drilled and hit hard ground. The ten men were finding it difficult to work the augur. Two well endowed women were selected because of their weight and put sitting on top of the auger to help it bite. These determined villagers had to dig five wells, before they succeeded in reaching safe water.

When we did a review of the work for our funders, the United States Agency for International Development, (USAID) we asked the people how life has changed for them. *"Since we have dug the well"*, the elders said *"we no longer lose any child or woman to crocodiles each year"*. That was certainly an unexpected outcome that we had not envisaged, but we did note that it was women and children who were involved in fetching water from the river! In our report write up, we informed USAID of this unexpected outcome.

Each year, our Water Department in the Diocese used to hire a bulldozer and dig a rain dam. One year, there was a dam dug just outside Bura village. The contractor was still at the dam, putting finishing touches to his work, when tremendous heavy rain began to fall up-country and lasted for twenty four hours. We watched in amazement as the seasonal river began to flood and the dam filled to the brim within two days. The dam walls were still settling and the contractor feared that it would burst, but it held. We were also surprised to see a water bird arriving to see what sweet morsels he could get from this new lake! How did the bird know so quickly that this was a new source of water? Was it pure chance that he was flying nearby?

Mamoud Tom and the Hole in the Wall gang

A Traditional Birth Attendant came early one morning saying that a young girl named Mariamu in Village 3 had been trying for hours to deliver and that she was now exhausted. She would have to be brought to Bura-Tana Health Centre. We drove up to the village and I stopped the jeep outside the house. The TBA entered the house, but I was surprised when she did not go in through the door but entered through a hole in the wall – the house was about to fall down. It was a sign of utter poverty. The house was falling down around the family. All I could think about was 'the Hole in the Wall gang!'

I waited in the Landcruiser vehicle with the engine running. The gentle purring of the big diesel engine must have done something, because after a short while, I heard the cry of a baby.

Sometime later, I told the story of Mariamu and her son to my nephews and one of them financed the building of a new house for the family, while the other sponsored the child through school. My grand nieces Yasmin Hogan and Cathy Burns supervised the building while they were with me for a summer. They employed the family as labourers in the work of building, so some money went directly into the family. Later on, Yasmin and her family sponsored the child who was called Mamoud Tom. He is now in primary school.

A further lesson in generosity

I was given a new appointment in December 2005 and went to say goodbye to the good people among whom I had lived for the best part of ten years. We had a Thanksgiving Mass and they suggested that I provide two goats for the feast. During the Mass, the various Catholic communities gave me gifts, particularly of clothing. This included a Safari suit which the local tailor had made. There were some shirts and trousers. They told me, "*We want to dress you well as you go home to your family. We want them to know that we looked after you and that we loved you*".

What a gift! A gift from the poorest of the poor! Although the shirts and trousers are China's best and only cost a few euros, they are worth much more than that to me because they are the widow's mite of the Gospel. A child was also brought up for blessing and they told me it would be my child and that they would rear her and educate her in my name. Sometimes we can just touch the hem of the Master's garment.

Time to say goodbye to Bura-Tana and start a new venture

I contacted my friend Peter Suttle who had lived with me in Bura-Tana for six years. Peter had not been back to visit in the three years since we had been last attacked. I felt he should put closure on our effort. I told him *'We went to Bura together and we should leave together. It's time to close the chapter'*. He agreed. I collected him in Nairobi and we spent three days visiting and saying good bye to the people. Peter and I returned back to Nairobi after our adventure in Tana River and were welcomed back by the very same Holy Rosary sisters who had sent us off nine years previously. How kind of them to remember us.

In 2004, I met Fr Peter Ndegwa in Nairobi who was waiting for his visa to enable him take up a new appointment in Ethiopia. I suggested that he join me in Tana River while he was waiting. He agreed to come and did not take up the appointment in Ethiopia. Much later on in the year, we were asked to start up a new parish in Wenje in the Tana River.

Wenje is near Ndera, where in 1887, members of our congregation started the first mainland parish in Kenya. It was to last less than a year and Br Achuel and Father Charles Grommenginger died soon after. In fact, Fr Charles died on the ship the M.V. Ethiopia while he was being shipped from Lamu to Zanzibar where there was a doctor. He is buried in Zanzibar.

As the Bishop said to me *"My people can't do it, you fellows know what to do. There is no house built yet, you will have to manage somehow"*. On January the 30th 2005, a group of us set off for Wenje. We had surveyed the area and had met some of the fifty Catholic families that attend the newly built church. However, there was no house for the priests. So we purchased a bit of land and set off in two heavily laden pick-up trucks. I borrowed all my old camping gear from St Mary's school.

In one day, we had to travel 100 kms and set up camp for about eight of us. To help us in the venture, we brought with us the local blacksmith Hassan, a local builder named Kamau, Peter Msafiri as driver, mechanic and general factotum and Anna Warimu as cook.

We pitched sufficient tents, made a makeshift shower, dug a latrine and laid out a suitable area as a kitchen. The kitchen table was made from an old door. It made a fine table with stout legs, cut from some suitable tree trunks. The kitchen had three walls made of canvas and a canvas roof. The toilet was a simple affair, a chair with a hole in the seat, set over a shallow trench and a bucket of sand and a small spade. Singing or whistling was recommended when using the toilet to ensure privacy! Shower facilities were set up under a nearby tree and you just had to turn on the tap of the shower bucket and to get water from a plastic tank set in the tree. The water was warm, having been heated by the hot sun during the day.

Seminarian Nicholas Mtua, who was also with us, said that we should celebrate Mass on that first evening. We invited a number of the church leaders, including the head of the women's group, the youth, choir, dancers, catechist and parish council. We celebrated Mass under a huge tree in our camp. Bush lamps gave us light and a simple kitchen table was to be our altar. It was to be a magical evening.

I spoke about the history of the area. How Brother Achuel and Fr Charles had travelled here with Monsignor De Courmont, Vicar Apostolic of Zanzibar and Fr Le Roy. They had first attempted to travel by boat up the Tana River but were stopped by lack of water at one point. On December the 29th 1887, they celebrated Mass and so the first mainland parish was canonically established in Kenya.

Fr Charles Grommenginger and Brother Achuel were left behind to build up the parish. However, during the rainy season, the Tana River began to flood so Charles and Achuel built themselves shelters up in the trees. Some time later, with tremendous difficulty, Br Achuel travelled by canoe and on foot to Mombasa with the alarming news that Fr Charles was near death. Le Roy rushed to the rescue and they brought Charles to Lamu, where he caught a ship, the MV Ethiopia on its way to Zanzibar where the only doctor in East Africa resided. Unfortunately, Fr Charles died on the journey. In his later career, Fr LeRoy was to become a famous author, an Archbishop and the world leader of the Spiritans.

Floods and malaria had defeated these intrepid missionaries. We knew we were part of history – a new beginning for the parish of St Joseph's of Ndera. After Mass, Anna Warimu, our cook, served up food for the sixteen of us and did us proud. That night, we named our camp Br Achuel's Camp, in memory of those early heroes. Within a few weeks, our camp began to take shape and life improved. A water pump and a large new tent were financed by my sister Helena and her husband Brian, and my brother Pat and his wife Erin.

Animals visit our camp

As days passed, our camp improved; each tent soon had solar lights and even a television and VCR in the dining area. The solar lights had advantages and disadvantages. One night, I woke up and found it hard to get back to sleep and was just lying on my bed. The soft welcome light of the solar lamp was on the outside of my tent. Then I noticed that there were some shadows passing by my tent. I looked and was amazed to see the shadow of a huge animal. It was gigantic; I could make out four legs, a stout body, ears and tusks! Could elephants have entered the camp! But I should not have worried; it was just a bush pig which had walked in between the light and the tent.

It was quite hot and during the nights some of my staff would sleep outside their tents. However, this custom did not last long, because, early one morning, our Arab supplier arrived by lorry from Mombasa. He had travelled through the relative cool of the night. He told us 'You have had visitors' and then we saw the spoor of lion in the sandy soil. A large male, with his mate and a cub had walked through the camp. The male lion had entered the kitchen area and had a look around. The lions left as silently as they had come. During the night, you could hear wild pigs foraging for food and frequently we had plains game like gazelles visiting us. We had brought a watchdog with us to keep guard, but the local Pokomo warned me that our dog would not last long as he was a visitor to the area. They suggested that I should have brought two or even three dogs, they would watch out for each other.

The crocodile has eaten our dog

Sometime later, we managed to get a Food for Work programme and we were given permission from the chief to cut saplings, which would enable us to make a stout fence around the camp. After visits from wild bush pigs and the lions, we felt a need for more security. We wondered how we would manage to stop the nearby villagers using a footpath running right through our camp. I got the idea of asking the Muslim villagers to build a fence beside their village. We marked out the area to be fenced; it was nearly two acres. We cut a footpath through the bush for the village and asked them to start on their fence. This would block their entry to use the short cut, but they did not seem to mind as they were already using the new footpath. No sooner had we completed the fence when the watchman told me that during the night some elephants had crossed the river and come up to our fence and walked along the side of it. We were glad we had the fence.

The camp was now fully functional and we began to use the Tana River as a means of transport. If we could get across to the far side of the river, it would save us a two hundred kilometres journey to one of our mission stations.

One Sunday afternoon, we were making the first launch of a boat in the river when we heard that Brandy, our watch dog, had disappeared. He had just been for a run with a student, who was walking the dog in return for his school fees. He had left Brandy off the chain as he ran him and the dog went ahead to the river. When the boy reached the river, he saw no sign of the dog. However, spoor along the river showed that a dog had gone to the river's edge and had been taken by a crocodile. That put an end to the launch of the boat! My two priest friends never ate the local delicacy, crocodile, after that. They said *"the crocodile has eaten our dog and we can't eat dog, so we can't eat crocodile any more"*.

Policemen teach us how to be generous.

The new Mission pickup truck had been involved in an accident and it was 'arrested' and impounded by the police. During the accident, a child was slightly injured. The child had run across the road because she was being chased by her mother. Peter and Dan, who were priests from Kenya, decided that I should be the one to go and get the car out of prison. They felt that the European had a better chance of getting the vehicle past inspection without having to pay a bribe. It was arranged that I would drive the car from Hola Police Station to the Vehicle Inspection centre at Garissa where it would be tested.

I went to the Station and met the Inspector. He gave me the keys of my car and introduced his two police officers, who would be escorting the vehicle. He asked me if I could oblige them by transporting a sick prisoner, who was going to the hospital for an examination for mental stability. This man had threatened to kill some of the policemen with a knife. He had already been jailed for this offence some years previous. I agreed and the police officers brought their prisoner in handcuffs. They asked me if I would help them by transporting their wives to Garissa. It was the end of the month and they hoped that there would be money in their bank accounts. The women could do some shopping.

We started on our journey. By now, we had a good load onboard and I thought about our back rear tyre. It was not one of the original tyres but came from a similar pick-up vehicle that we had. The tyre was not new and I wondered would it pass the inspection? Fortunately, after about 150 kms, we had a puncture in the very wheel about which I had some doubt.

As we entered Garissa town, I suggested to the officers that we should leave the wheel into the service station and have the puncture repaired. It would be a long journey home, their women were with them and they agreed. So, now the dodgy tyre would not be going for the inspection - first problem solved.

We brought our patient to the hospital for examination only to be told that the doctor would not be present for two or three days. There was nothing for it but to bring our patient to the holding cells in the local police post. When we went there and handed over our prisoner patient, we found that food for the day had already been served to the other prisoners, thus our man would have a hungry day and a hungrier night! I then saw the policemen go and purchase a litre of milk and half a loaf of bread which they gave to our patient. I was impressed by their kindness, they had little money and they did not know if they would find money in the bank, yet they fed this prisoner.

The officers asked if we could not first go to the bank to enable them to get their salaries. I agreed and I enquired if I could drive to the mission compound and see the Bishop. Off we went on our separate journeys and I took the opportunity to replace a broken fuse, so that the horn would sound. I was now all set for the vehicle inspection and went and collected the police officers, who were disappointed to find no money in their accounts. The pick-up truck passed the inspection with flying colours, we collected our spare wheel and set off on the long journey home, first to Hola and then I would continue on to Wenje on my own. We would be travelling home during the dark but I was not worried as my two escorts were armed. I knew that they would protect their wives and the baby. Later on, I wrote to the commanding officer and asked him to note his officer's generosity in their personal files. I felt it would be good to have on their record.

More visitors to our camp and time to return home

During Easter 2005, we had a number of visitors and we slaughtered a goat to welcome them. Fr Everest Chao, the Provincial of the East African Province came to visit Peter and Dan while Fr Pat Palmer, Provincial of Ireland, came to see me. We wondered how they would survive under canvas, since none of them had ever camped out before. However, we shouldn't have been concerned as they found the camp very comfortable. They were impressed with the ingenuity which we had used in setting up Brother Achuel's Camp. Everest wrote up an account of his visit and we received unexpected publicity.

One hot afternoon, the temperature had reached 43ºC and we could not go into the tents, as they were like ovens at that time of the day. As we sat in the shade of a tree, Pat asked me if I would consider returning to Ireland. The post would be Assistant Director of Spiritan Asylum Services Initiative. SPIRASI was our Millennium Project and it is unique in being the only centre on the island of Ireland which offers care to survivors of torture. I was surprised to be asked, to say the least and requested some time to consider. I was given a year to decide. I had previously no intention of returning to Ireland, however, on consideration and on the advice of my doctor, I agreed.

In January 2nd 2006, I took up the position offered. My years in Africa had been exciting, fulfilling and challenging and I had made many friends. I left with mixed feelings. I had lived more than half of my life in Kenya and was about to return to my homeland. What lay in store for me?